I0091269

FSS MONOGRAPH SERIES 3

DEMOCRATIC ASSISTANCE TO POST-CONFLICT ETHIOPIA
Impact and Limitations

Dessalegn Rahmato
Forum for Social Studies
and
Meheret Ayenew
Faculty of Business and Economics
Addis Ababa University

Forum for Social Studies
Addis Ababa

The opinions expressed in this publication are those of the authors and do not necessarily reflect the views of FSS or its Board of Advisors.

Financial support for the printing of this publication was provided by the ROYAL NORWEGIAN EMBASSY for which we are grateful.

ISBN: 1-904855-65-2
ISBN-13: 978-1-904855-65-1
Copyright: © The Authors and Forum for Social Studies 2004

TABLE OF CONTENTS

Tables

Figure

Acknowledgements

We would like to thank all government officials, staff of human rights groups and officials of donor agencies who provided us information and who were kind enough to sit for interviews and to answer our questions. Without their cooperation this study would not have been completed. We would also like to thank all participants of the brainstorming workshop held on 28 October 2003 to discuss the preliminary findings of the study; their critical comments were very valuable to us.

Finally, our sincere appreciation to our research assistant, Fassil Yenealem, who was diligent and hardworking, who spared no effort in tracking down sources of information and documents, and who played a very important supporting role in the preparation of the study.

i

Acronyms

AACC	=	Addis Ababa Chamber of Commerce
AAPO	=	All-Amhara People's Organization
AAI	=	African-American Institute
ACP	=	African, Caribbean and Pacific [Countries]
ADLI	=	Agricultural Development Led Industrialization
AI	=	Amnesty International
AIDA	=	Accessible Information on Development Activities
ALF	=	Afar Liberation Front
ANDM	=	Amhara National Democratic Movement
APAP	=	Action Professionals Association for the People
AW	=	Africa Watch
CEC	=	Commission of the European Communities
CETU	=	Confederation of Ethiopian Trade Unions
CIDA	=	Canadian International Development Agency
CLCBS	=	Center for Local Capacity Building and Studies
CRDA	=	Christian Relief and Development Association
CSA	=	Central Statistical Authority
DBS	=	Direct Budget Support
DEU	=	Donor Election Unit
DFID	=	Department for International Development
DAG	=	Donor Assistant Group
DPPC	=	Disaster Prevention and Preparedness Commission
EC(D)	=	European Commission (Delegation)
ECSEC	=	Eneweyay Civic and Social Education Center
EDP	=	Ethiopian Democratic Party
EEA	=	Ethiopian Economic Association
EEPRI	=	Ethiopian Economic Policy Research Institute
EFJA	=	Ethiopian Free Press Journalists Association
EH	=	Ethiopian Herald
EHRCO	=	Ethiopian Human Rights Council
EMA	=	Educational Media Agency

EMWA	=	Ethiopian Media Women Association
ENCONEL	=	Ethiopian Non-Governmental Organizations Consortium for Elections
EPRDF	=	Ethiopian Peoples Revolutionary Democratic Front
ESP	=	Ye-Ethiopia Serategnoch Party
EU	=	European Union
EWLA	=	Ethiopian Women Lawyers Association
FAO	=	Food and Agricultural Organization
FDRE	=	Federal Democratic Republic of Ethiopia
FEAC	=	Federal Ethics and Anti-Corruption Commission
FES	=	Friedrich Ebert Stiftung
FSS	=	Forum for Social Studies
GDP	=	Gross Domestic Product
HIPC	=	Highly Indebted Poor Countries
HoF	=	House of Federation
HPR	=	House of Peoples Representatives
HRW	=	Human Rights Watch
IFEX	=	International Freedom of Expression and Exchange
IFHR	=	International Federation of Human Rights
IMF	=	International Monetary Fund
IPI	=	International Press Institute
IPU	=	Inter-Parliamentary Union
JTU	=	Justice Training Unit
MMTI	=	Mass Media Training Institute
MoE	=	Ministry of Education
MoI	=	Ministry of Information
MoJ	=	Ministry of Justice
NDI	=	National Democratic Institute
NEB	=	National Electoral Board
NGO	=	Non-Government Organization
NORAD	=	Norwegian Aid
ODA	=	Official Development Assistance
OECD	=	Organization for Economic Cooperation and Development

OLF	=	Oromo Liberation Front
ONC	=	Oromo National Congress
OPDO	=	Oromo People's Democratic Organization
PDRE	=	People's Democratic Republic of Ethiopia
PMAC	=	Provisional Military Administrative Council
SAHRE	=	Society for the Advancement of Human Rights
SAP	=	Structural Adjustment Program
SDPRP	=	Sustainable Development and Poverty Reduction Program
SEPDC	=	South Ethiopia Peoples' Democratic Coalition
TGE	=	Transitional Government of Ethiopia
TPLF	=	Tigrai People's Liberation Front
UK	=	United Kingdom
UNDP	=	United Nations Development Programme
UNESCO	=	United Nations Educational, Scientific & Cultural Organization
UNICEF	=	United Nations Children's Fund
UNMEE	=	United Nations Mission in Ethiopia and Eritrea
US	=	United States
USAID	=	United States Agency for International Development
WB	=	World Bank
WFP	=	World Food Programme
WHO	=	World Health Organization
WPE	=	Worker's Party of Ethiopia

DEMOCRATIC ASSISTANCE TO POST-CONFLICT ETHIOPIA
Impact and Limitations

Dessalegn Rahmato and Meheret Ayenew

Abstract

There is a long history of donor relationship with Ethiopia going back at least to the early 1940s. Since then, the number of bi- and multi-lateral donors providing assistance to the country has grown substantially. At present, the U.S., Japan and the Scandinavian countries are the major bilateral donors, while the World Bank, the EU and agencies in the UN system provide the bulk of the multilateral assistance. The international assistance that was offered to the country with the change of regime may be grouped into three categories: a) development assistance; b) humanitarian assistance; and c) assistance for democratization and good governance.

Ethiopia has conducted a number of elections in the post-conflict period, the last one being in 2000. At present, the country is bracing itself for a third round of national elections in 2005. A comparison of election costs for selected African countries with Ethiopia shows that the cost of elections in Ethiopia has been quite low given the country's enormous size and its lack of experience in running democratic elections. Ethiopia has received considerable international electoral assistance since 1991 and such assistance has strengthened the capacity of the National Electoral Board and civil society and human rights organizations in monitoring and supervising elections. Donor assistance has also been provided to political parties to make the electoral process more competitive. However, the impact of such assistance in democratizing the election process has been limited because the ruling party has failed to broaden its political power base and provide a level playing field for all contestants.

Human rights and advocacy organizations began to be established for the first time in the country following the fall of the Derg and the change of government. This has meant that the human rights record of the present government has been more systematically monitored and rights violations more extensively compiled than at any time in the past. Donor assistance to human rights has primarily been financial assistance to advocacy organizations on the one hand, and financial support as well as training and technical support to government institutions on the other. Assistance has been provided for: a) preparatory work for setting up a government human right commission and ombudsman institution; b) reform of legal institutions, and training of law enforcement agencies; c) support to legislative bodies and training of legislators; d) financial support to civil society organizations active in monitoring human rights, human rights protection and advocacy.

One of the first acts of the Transitional Government was to enact a press law, which turned out to have a dramatic impact on the country's media. At present, there are a large number of private papers published regularly. However, the free press is faced by a host of problems: structural, economic, and professional. International assistance to the media (both public as well as private) has been limited in scope, and relatively insignificant in terms of its impact. International donors have failed to make a strategic intervention in the media sector and have been limited to low level support with only limited results.

Donor assistance to the democratization process in Ethiopia has been comparatively limited. In contrast, donors have invested heavily in the humanitarian and relief effort on the one hand, and in the socio-economic development sectors on the other. Assistance to both sectors has been growing in the last ten years, and in particular assistance to the humanitarian sector has been increasing markedly in this period.

On the other hand, financial support to civil society, especially local human rights and advocacy organizations, has been instrumental in enabling the growth of the voluntary sector in the country. Without such *support, civil society would have faced serious difficulties, and its achievements, especially in the areas of human rights monitoring, training and advocacy, would have been more limited. On the other hand, the impact of international assistance on the democratization process in this country has been quite limited. The achievements registered to date in the areas of elections, human rights and press freedom have primarily been a product of local initiative, local organizations, and struggles by stakeholders.*

Preface

There are a few points that we wish to raise here to put this work in proper context and to give the reader a better understanding of the circumstances under which the work was prepared.

This work is part of a research project covering eight countries and intended to look into the role and effectiveness of international assistance in supporting the process of democratization in post-conflict situations[1]. The project was sponsored by the Netherlands Institute of International Relations based in The Hague. The countries in question, all of which have emerged from a period of destructive conflict within the last two or so decades, include Ethiopia, Uganda, Rwanda, Mozambique and Sierra Leone in Africa, Guatemala and El Salvador in Central America, and Cambodia in Asia. The study was launched in May 2003 and was planned to be completed in November of the same year. The timeframe for our study is 1991 to mid-2003.

The research framework as well as the specific content of the study was defined by the Institute, which also selected the countries in which the investigation was to be undertaken. The project was designed to focus on three areas that were thought to constitute critical components of democracy, namely, elections, human rights, and the media. An important issue that was to be investigated was whether or not donor assistance has contributed to the development of sustainable and effective electoral, media and human rights institutions in post-conflict societies.

Obviously, the study would have been structured differently if the framework and content were defined at the outset by the present authors themselves. This is not meant to imply a criticism of the Netherlands Institute. The Institute had to formulate a common framework for comparative purposes and to satisfy its own specific objectives, one of which was gaining a better understanding of the impact of international

---

[1] For the preliminary definition of the research project see the Netherlands Institute of International Relations, "Research Framework (Workshop Version, 1 May 2003)", The Hague.

assistance and how it can be improved to make a sustainable contribution to the process of democratization in post-conflict societies. Secondly, the authors were faced with several limitations, of which the lack of adequate information, in particular from donor agencies, and the time available to investigate the broad subjects identified in the research framework were the most serious. Democratization is a complex process, and the past has an important impact on the present. However, the research did not provide sufficient opportunity to investigate in depth Ethiopia's recent political past. The project defined the post-conflict period as "the phase beginning with the signing of the peace agreement or the end of the violent conflict".

As far as we know, this is the first study to examine the role and effectiveness of international assistance on the democratization process in Ethiopia. The practice in this country up to now has been for donors to examine the performance of government and non-government institutions; we have reversed the spot light, focusing instead on donors and the impact of their assistance. We hope this will stimulate serious debate and will encourage more in-depth studies of a similar nature in the future. The work is a slightly revised version of the draft we submitted to the Netherlands Institute for publication. That draft contains a more detailed list of specific recommendations to donors (which we have taken out from the present work).

Dessalegn Rahmato
Meheret Ayenew
April 2004

I. COUNTRY INTRODUCTION

1. Background

With a population estimated in 2000 to be more than 64 million and a land area of 1.13 million km^2, Ethiopia is one of the largest countries in Sub-Saharan Africa. It has a relatively high population density, ranging from 150 persons/km^2 in Wollo in the northeast of the country to over 300 persons/km^2 in parts of south-central Ethiopia. The population is estimated to be growing at 3 percent per year, and the demographic profile reflects the preponderance of the young, with those below twenty-five years of age making up nearly two-thirds of the total population (CSA 1999a). Urbanization is very low, and only 15 percent of the population lives in urban centers, which makes the country one of the least urbanized in the world.

The country is one of the poorest in the world, ranked 169 out of 175 in UNDP's latest *Human Development Report* (2003b). Per capita income is the lowest in Sub-Saharan Africa, and average food consumption per capita per day is estimated to be less than 70 percent of internationally accepted standards (World Bank 2000). According to FAO reports, Ethiopia is one of the ten hungriest nations in the world (2001), and frequent food crises, including virulent famines, have brought suffering and devastation to the rural population all through the last half century. There is sufficient evidence that over the last fifty years, poverty, and in particular rural poverty, has been growing in severity and magnitude, and that the country's agriculture, which is the dominant sector of the economy serving as the main means of livelihood for the overwhelming majority of the population, has been in structural decline. This is evidenced by recurrent incidents of mass starvation and high levels of livelihood as well as ecological vulnerability (Dessalegn 2003a).

The economy is dominantly rural, and, according to recent CSA (1999b) figures, the agricultural sector accounts for 81 percent of total employment and 84 percent of total exports. Agriculture's contribution to GDP is high but has been falling since the 1960s when it contributed 65 percent, while at the end of the 1990s this had decreased to a little over 45 percent (Befekadu and Berhanu 2000). Agriculture consists overwhelmingly of smallholder peasant cultivation producing a range of food crops primarily for own consumption using traditional farming practices. Due to stagnant land and labour productivity, food production has failed to keep pace with population growth. Similarly, due to population growth and the

1

scarcity of arable land reserves, per capita farm plots are small and getting smaller, and the fertility of the land is diminishing continuously. There are those who have argued that unless a determined shift in economic policy towards greater industrialization is forthcoming, the prospects for the viability of Ethiopian agriculture and the sustainability of the environmental resources will be in doubt in the decades ahead (Dessalegn 2003a).

The modern sector of the economy consists of a large service sector and a small industrial base. Manufacturing enterprises, both public and private, produce a small range of consumer goods predominantly for the local market; however, since the economic liberalization of the early 1990s they have had to compete, often unsuccessfully, with products flooding into the country from the booming economies of east and south Asia. Manufacturing industry in Ethiopia is in very poor state because it employs obsolete technology, and because many of the enterprises were established in the 1960s and are today in a decrepit condition. Industry accounts for 11 percent of total exports and two percent of total employment. There has been only limited investment in the past in basic infrastructure and thus surface transport, communications, electric power, and water supply are little developed. However, there has been some progress in this regard since the 1980s, although there is a long way to go before the country can have an efficient modern transport and communications infrastructure. Persistent poverty and livelihood insecurity over the last half century, brought on by underdevelopment, civil conflict, natural resource degradation, high population growth and frequent environment crises, have given rise to increasing poverty and permanent food insecurity, which from time to time has led to devastating famines.

Ethiopia's political history in the last four decades has been one of upheaval and radical change. In this period, the country has had three radically different political regimes involving in each case economic, legal and administrative reorganization, leading to a great deal of institutional instability[1].

Until the mid-1970s, the country was ruled by an absolute monarchy, with political power concentrated in the hands of Emperor Haile Selassie, and economic power in the hands of a class of landed nobility and local gentry which between them owned a preponderant

---

[1] The discussion in this Chapter is based on the personal experience of the authors as well as the following works: for the period up to end of the 1980s: Andargachew 1993, Clapham 1988, Gilkes 1975, Markakis 1974; for the 1990s and after: Merera 2003;Pausewang et al. 2002, and Tronvoll 2000.

share of the country's productive resources. The nobility and gentry controlled a major portion of the country's arable land, which was parceled out and worked by a class of poor tenant farmers. Haile Selassie's regime, which lasted from 1930 to 1974, with a brief period of Italian colonial rule (1935-41), was relatively stable and the period fairly peaceful for a majority of the population. The violent conflicts that were to bring large-scale destruction and loss of lives, and serious instability and disorder in the country are, by and large, a legacy of the post- Imperial period. The one regional uprising which erupted in the first half of the 1960s and which the Imperial regime was unable to put down was that in Eritrea, which was then a province of the country. While by the end of the Imperial regime this regional conflict had become an established liberation movement, it was successfully contained all through the 1960s and early '70s, with limited effect on the daily lives of a majority of the Eritrean population.

The modernization of the state under the Imperial regime was not accompanied by the democratization of the polity, nevertheless, the Emperor did establish a parliament, provide a written constitution (in 1931, revised in 1955), and introduce universal suffrage and a national electoral system. Elections to the lower House of Parliament were held every five years from 1957 onwards, however, since political parties were not allowed electoral seats were contested on individual basis. Parliament had little effective power but it debated legislation and acted as a sounding board. Absolute monarchy did not tolerate dissent or criticism, and the constitution affirmed that the Emperor ruled by divine right. Neither civil society organizations (other than customary self-help and burial societies) nor an independent media were allowed.

The Provisional Military Administrative Council (PMAC), or Derg, which seized power by overthrowing the monarchy in 1974, switched the country's diplomatic alliance towards the Soviet bloc, and embarked on the disastrous road of "socialization" of the country's polity and economy. The earliest reform which subsequently was to be the cornerstone of agricultural collectivization was the radical land reform of 1975. This effectively ended landlordism in the country, emancipating millions of peasants from the control of the propertied classes. However, land was to be state property and the peasant had only usufruct rights over it. Subsequent reforms eroded the benefits of the land reform, preparing the way for the socialization of agriculture. In the 1980s, partly as a response to the devastating famine and environmental shocks, the Derg embarked upon a massive program of resettlement and villagization involving millions of peasants. The popularity and good will it had gained from the peasantry as a result of its effective measures against the propertied classes and the distribution of land evaporated as the government turned more and more towards hard line Stalinist reform policies.

The Derg's democratic pretensions only became apparent some twelve years after it had seized power. In 1987, it introduced a constitution which vested power in the National Assembly. However, in line with the accepted formula of Soviet bloc countries, the Derg established a party in the Leninist tradition, called the Serategnoch Party of Ethiopia (ESP) as the ruling party of the country. Effective power remained in the hands of Colonel Mengistu Haile Mariam, the military dictator, and a small coterie of his advisors who were appointed as the leading officials of the Party. Elections to the Assembly were held subsequently, but the seats were contested only by ESP cadres, and the outcome was decided long before the formal ballots were cast. The Derg was perhaps the most despotic and the most brutal regime in the country's history. Thousands of people were executed without trial, hundreds of thousands were thrown in jail on trumped up charges, and innumerable men and women were forced to flee the country for fear of arrest, persecution or execution.

2. Conflict History

Though their roots go much further back in the country's troubled history, the violent conflicts which engulfed the country all through the 1980s started in the post-Imperial period and escalated as a response to the unpopular policies of the Derg. These conflicts consisted of a feeble attempt at armed resistance by what the Derg called "the counter-revolution" (remnants of the propertied classes and their allies on the one hand, and radical opponents of the Derg on the other), war with neighboring Somalia, the Eritrean independence movement, and ethnic-based insurgency, first in the northwest of the country but later in western Ethiopia. The war with Somalia, which claimed a large swathe of Ethiopian territory, was humiliating for the Derg, and it was able to finally drive back the Somalia invasion forces, which had over-run a considerable part of eastern Ethiopia, with the active involvement of Cuban troops and large-scale Soviet arms airlift. The Eritrean independence struggle, which was now able to field a large fighting force and engage the Derg in conventional warfare, threatened to over-run Eritrea at any moment, hence the Derg was forced to commit a considerable portion of its military force and resources to defend the province. From the latter part of the 1970s, the

Tigrai People's Liberation Front (TPLF), which was fighting the Derg in the northwest of the country, grew to be a strong force to contend with. Other ethnic-based insurgencies included the Afar Liberation Front(ALF) in the northeast and the Oromo Liberation Front (OLF) in the southwest, and an Islamic movement in the southeast.

While on all the fronts the fighting was conducted between one armed force and another, there were spillover effects in which civilian populations were caught in the middle. But unlike civil conflicts in some countries in Africa (eg. Sierra Leone, Liberia, the Congo) or central America, there were few *deliberate* attempts on the part of one side or another to extend the war to non-combatants. Thus genocide, large-scale massacres, or acts of mass terror against civilian populations during the war were fairly limited. Engaged on many fronts, and exhausted by continuous warfare that had been going on since the second half of the 1970s, the Derg's army began to crumble in the latter part of the 1980s. Due to high rates of attrition, a large part of the army was made up of young peasants forcibly recruited, and these had neither the training nor the stomach to fight what appeared to be an endless war. Moreover, the restructuring of the military apparatus by the Derg had been accompanied by the politicization, Soviet style, of the military personnel. Alongside the regular hierarchy of non-commissioned and commissioned officers were appointed political cadres recruited very frequently from the lower ranks who, as activists of the ruling party, ESP, were given far more importance than the officer corps. This was to be one of the most important causes of low morale within the Derg army.

The anti-Derg forces, subsequently united into a coalition of ethnic-based parties called the Ethiopian People's Revolutionary Democratic Front (EPRDF), with the TPLF as the dominant partner, intensified their offensive against government forces towards the end of the 1980s, winning ground and advancing on Addis Ababa rapidly. As the Derg army continued to disintegrate, and the government increasingly lost all support from the public, in particular the peasantry, the insurgents' offensive met with little resistance. In mid-May 1991, with the rebels almost at the gates of the capital, Mengistu Haile Mariam fled the country for exile in Zimbabwe. There was an attempt to bring together all the rebel groups and the Derg at the short-lived London Peace Conference in early May 1991, with the U.S. playing an active role to broker a peace deal, but this flopped because the Derg was collapsing at that very moment and the rebels were at the gates of the capital. The main beneficiary of the aborted Conference was the EPRDF, which gained the support of Washington and which was to provide it a measure of legitimacy among Western powers. The EPRDF forces finally entered Addis Ababa on 28 May, with the Eritrean liberation forces capturing Asmara soon after. This brought to an end over a decade and half of brutal military dictatorship. While there was confusion and uncertainty among large sections of the public with regard to the future, it was everyone's hope that the overthrow of the Derg would usher in a time of peace and stability.

The EPRDF's immediate objective after seizing power was to bring about peace and public order. This was a welcome initiative, for after nearly two decades of insurgency and civil conflict, there was an overwhelming desire on the part of the public for an end to hostilities and civil discord. But the most important reform agenda of the new rulers was to destroy the apparatus of state built up under the Derg, to restructure the country and its civil administration along ethnic lines, and to establish ethnicity as the defining principle of political, social and economic discourse. As part of this endeavor, EPRDF convened a "Peace and Democracy Conference" a month after assuming power in which twenty-nine ethnic-based political groups, most of which hastily organized for the occasion a week or two earlier, participated. The conference, which was dominated by EPRDF, and through it the TPLF, endorsed a Charter for the transitional period, and approved the establishment of the Transitional Government of Ethiopia with an interim legislative body in which the EPRDF, and the Oromo Liberation Front were heavily represented. It also approved the holding of a UN-supervised referendum in Eritrea to formalize its separation from Ethiopia. With the subsequent independence of Eritrea, Ethiopia lost its outlet to the sea. The Charter affirmed respect for the law, protection of human rights, and equality of all ethnic nationalities which had the right to self-determination but which were to be part of a federal Ethiopia (TGE 1991).

Following the setting-up of the Transitional Government, there were a number of important political developments. The country's administrative map was redrawn along ethnic lines and "Regional States" for each of the major nationalities were created. These Regional States were given wide administrative and legislative power. The goal was to be the devolution of power within a federal framework. In 1992, local and regional elections were held throughout the country. The elections were monitored both by local and foreign observers. Ethnic federalism was further formalized by the drafting of a Constitution in 1994 following elections that were held to the Constituent Assembly whose job was to ratify the Constitution. The

Constitution establishes a federal state, the component elements of which were "nations, nationalities and peoples". It endorses respect for human rights, the rule of law, and a multi-party electoral regime. There were federal parliamentary and Regional elections in 1995 and five years later in 2000 on the one hand, and local council elections in 2001 on the other. In all instances, foreign observers were allowed to monitor the balloting process.

3. The Elusive Peace

The establishment of peace and public order in the country following the fall of the Derg proved to be a difficult undertaking. Due to many years of civil war, both internally and also among ethnic and political divisions in the neighboring countries of the Horn, there was a large inflow of arms into Ethiopia as well as the region as a whole. Moreover, the defeated and subsequently disbanded Derg army, numbering over 200,000 soldiers, many of whom still in possession of their arms, posed a serious threat to public order. The initial euphoria and partnership among the many small and unstable ethnic political groups that initially made up the EPRDF coalition did not last long, and soon the political process became polarized.

There were sporadic armed hostilities in several parts of the country as well as widespread armed robbery perpetrated by some of the disbanded soldiers and armed political groups. On the other hand, the government began to forcibly suppress first the OLF and later other smaller groups (such as the All-Amhara People's Organization and the Afar Liberation Front), which had decided to pull out of the coalition. Moreover, due in part what to many seemed to be the government's encouragement for "ethnic separation" and in part to zealous activism of party militants in the Regions, there were several incidents of communal violence in which many people on the wrong side of the ethnic divide lost their lives; a considerable number of people were displaced and a lot of property was destroyed in these conflicts.

Finally, there was the war with Eritrea, which came to a head following border incursions by the latter in 1998 (see Tekeste and Tronvoll 2000). Arguably the most senseless conflict in recent Africa history, the war placed an enormous burden on both countries which, in aggregate, lost tens of thousand of lives and caused immense suffering. Defense spending in Ethiopia went up sharply, resources that were earmarked for development and infrastructure were shifted to support the war, and the country's foreign exchange reserves were

7

depleted. The human toll on the Ethiopian side includes 300,000 internally displaced persons, 100,000 nationals deported from Eritrea, and 36,000 militia killed in the fighting (World Bank 2002). Comparable figures on the Eritrean side are not available though UNMEE notes that 350,000 Eritreans were displaced by the war (UNMEE website). The peace accords which were crafted in Algiers and which called for the cessation of armed hostilities were signed by both countries in 2000, and subsequently both agreed to seek arbitration on the border issue by an independent body. This led to the establishment of an independent Eritrea-Ethiopia Border Commission which began to hear evidence in The Hague in 2001. The peace accords also led to the establishment of UNMEE which was mandated to monitor the ceasefire and to liaise with the two parties. The war has had a damaging impact on the local economy as a whole, reducing private as well as public sector investment, slowing down business activity, and contributing to growing unemployment in the urban areas and elsewhere (EEA 2002).

The political changes briefly sketched above were accompanied by equally dramatic changes in the economic sphere. The Imperial regime promoted what may be termed a "mixed economy" made up of public, private and joint enterprises. The public sector was the dominant sector in the economy, but that was largely because of the relative weakness of the private sector rather than a conscious policy in favor of public enterprises. The private sector was made up of foreign and local capital, but the latter was overshadowed by the former. The country suffered from limited development of basic infrastructure and lacked a sufficiently large skilled labor force, and as a result the flow of foreign investment into the country was limited. On the other hand, the regime pursued a pragmatic economic policy, had a fairly well-crafted legal infrastructure ensuring protection for private investment, and generous incentives to attract foreign capital.

The Derg, which for some fifteen years was bent on building up a Soviet-style "command" economy, nationalized all productive resources and enterprises, including land, rental houses, foreign as well as local investments, and decimated the private sector. The pursuit of the full "socialization" of the economy was undertaken aggressively in the 1980s through the expansion of state enterprises in the manufacturing, commercial and retail sectors on the one hand and the collectivization of agriculture and villagization of the rural population on the other. By the beginning of 1990s, the combination of ill-advised and ideologically driven economic policy and a decade and half of war and violent conflict had resulted in the extreme

8

running down of the country's physical and human capital, and infrastructure.

The present government inherited a devastated economy and massive levels of poverty and unemployment. Its first task, soon after assuming power, was to launch a program of reconstruction on the one hand, and introduce reform measures to liberalize the command economy on the other. Encouraged by the World Bank and IMF, the government adopted a structural adjustment program (SAP) in 1992 which involved the devaluation of the currency, liberalization of trade, deregulation of labor and wages, and privatization of public enterprises. These reform measures had mixed results: on the negative side were sharp price rises of consumer goods and severe pressure on poor and low-income families on the one hand, and increasing unemployment on the other; on the positive side were stabilization of the macro-economic environment. There was a respectable rate of economic growth in the first five years with overall growth reaching 6 to 7 percent according to government figures, but opinion is divided on whether the main contributing factors were the SAP reforms, fortuitous circumstances, or a combination of both.

The government has made a commitment to pursue a policy of free market economy, but there are contradictory elements in the development measures it has pursued and in the reforms it has failed to undertake; some of these decisions are ideologically driven. Until recently, the government did not show a strong desire to create a favorable environment for the private sector, which was placed under pressure by high taxes, hostile attitudes from government functionaries, and a stifling bureaucracy. To this day, "para-statal" enterprises, owned and operated by the ruling Regional Parties, enjoy favorable status from government, and a competitive advantage vis-à-vis the private sector. The development strategy adopted since the mid-1990s, known as ADLI (Agricultural Development-Led Industrialization), which envisages peasant-based agriculture as the engine of growth, is based not on a sound assessment of the potential of the sector (which is limited) but reflects the bias of decision-makers. This strategy, pursued since the mid-1990s, has had poor results and has led to the neglect of the urban economy and the manufacturing sector (Befekadu, Berhanu and Getahun 2001).

Table 1.1 below provides a comparative picture of the similarities and differences of the three regimes under discussion on the basis of five "measures of democratization".

9

Table 1.1 **Comparative Political Profile of the Three Regimes**

Criteria	Imperial Regime 1941-74	Derg Regime 1974-91	EPRDF Regime 1991-2002
State Form	Absolute Monarchy; Unitary state	Marxist-Leninist; Unitary state	Ethnic Federalist state
Parties	No parties allowed; elections individual	Single Leninist party system	Multi-party elections allowed
Media/Press	Government media mainly; 1 private radio station	Government media only; highly restricted	Government media and independent press
Civil Society Organizations	CSOs highly restricted; some professional associations allowed	CSOs not allowed except inter'al NGOs; customary ones under pressure	CSOs allowed; growing number inc. advocacy and human rights ones.
Economy	Mixed economy; pragmatic policy	State or command economy; policy ideologically driven	Restricted market economy; policy ideologically driven

Source: Compiled by the authors

4. Post-Conflict Assistance

There is a long history of donor relationship with Ethiopia going back at least to the early 1940s. Initially, the main bilateral assistance came from a few countries, notably the U.S., Britain and Sweden, and multilateral assistance from the World Bank, FAO, WHO and UNESCO. Since then, the number of bi- and multi-lateral donors providing assistance to the country has grown substantially. At present, the U.S., Japan and the Scandinavian countries are the major bilateral donors, while the World Bank, the EU and agencies in the UN system provide the bulk of the multilateral assistance. In the 980s, at the time of the military regime, Soviet bloc countries provided substantial assistance, both military and economic. Interestingly enough, the Imperial regime did also benefit from economic assistance from the Soviet Union despite the obvious differences in political orientation between them. The relationship between the donors and the country has gone through cycles: many years of amicable relationship followed by years of friction and tension. During the Imperial regime, there was a slight falling off between the government and the donors towards the end of the 1960s when the latter were disappointed with the lack of progress in economic and political reforms. During the military government, the major donor countries such the U.S. withdrew their development support, though they continued to be significant actors in the area of humanitarian assistance. The Derg's Stalinist policies and its atrocious human rights record were cited as reasons for disengaging from the country. However, many European countries, the EC, as well as all of the multi-lateral donors continued to play active roles in the country.

The new government has enjoyed considerable goodwill from the international donor community from the moment it assumed power. The military dictatorship it had replaced was unpopular among many Western powers, in particular the U.S. and its European allies, and there was great relief that it had finally been successfully overthrown. As the collapse of the Derg became imminent, the leaders of the rebel movement had quietly abandoned their hard-line Marxist-Leninist ideology and were keen to adopt electoral politics and a free market economy. This and their eagerness to listen to the advice of U.S. officials gained the new leaders a lot of friends within the donor community.

The initial economic program that was adopted by the transitional government (TGE 1992b) was seen as sufficient proof that this was a government that the Western powers could do "business with". The World Bank and IMF were eager to have the TGE implement wide ranging structural reforms, in return for which they were to provide loans, grants and aid for reconstruction, while the bilateral donor agencies were ready to offer development assistance as well as aid for democratization and good governance. As noted above, it was not long before coming to power that the new rulers implemented a structural adjustment program which won them considerable support not just from the international financial institutions but also from the U.S., the EC and other significant donors.

But the problems facing the country and the new government are immense and the assistance required quite complex. To begin with, there had been considerable destruction of infrastructure, social services, and the running down of management capacity in the course of the long civil war, and it was thus necessary to invest in reconstruction if the country was to embark on development activity. Secondly, the new regime was confronted with a colossal human disaster: in the period up to the mid-1990s, there were over two million "displaced" persons who were without means, without employment, and some of whom posed a serious threat to public security as well as to the political stability of the government itself.

More recently, donors were at odds with the Federal government over issues relating to the conflict with Eritrea, and currently relating to the border demarcations. There are also other outstanding issues, such as the country's debt burden, economic liberalization, and the problems associated with recurrent food crises and famines that cause disagreement between one and the other. On the other hand, the government's recently completed poverty reduction strategy program, which was submitted to the international financial institutions as part of the debt relief (or HIPC) initiative, has promoted a notable degree of harmony between it and the donor community.

But the cycle of boom and bust in Ethio-donor relations, and the response of donors over the years have also been influenced by international events, geopolitical considerations and other contingent factors. First, Ethiopia is a big country within the Horn (or Greater Horn) of Africa, and the international community does not want the country to collapse or plunge into civil war because this would have a spillover effect on the Horn countries leading to their political destabilization. Moreover, the growth of "Islamic fundamentalism", particularly in the Sudan, Ethiopia's neighbor, has led the U.S. and others to value Ethiopia's friendship. Thirdly, the U.S.-led war in Afghanistan and Iraq, and the current campaign against "international terrorism" have been a godsend, as it were, to the country: Ethiopia supported the American effort in each instance and has been rewarded in return by generous humanitarian and other support by Washington, which now considers the country as a "frontline state" in the war against terrorism.

The international assistance that was offered to the country with the change of regime may be grouped into three categories: a) development assistance; b) humanitarian assistance; and c) assistance for democratization and good governance. Unfortunately figures for the last category are difficult to get access to, though the evidence that is available suggests that it is on a much smaller scale compared to the other two.

a. Development Assistance

A comprehensive picture of the official development assistance (ODA) to the country from 1997 to 2003 is provided by a recent report prepared by UNDP (2003a), and in what follows we shall present a summary of the findings. ODA here includes humanitarian and relief assistance, though not assistance to democratization and governance. But a few words on ODA data sources and the level of external assistance to the country is in order here.

First let us look at the data sources. There are three major sources of ODA flows to developing countries and we have looked at all three. These are the UNDP, OECD's *International Development Statistics 2003* which provides data on aid flows to developing countries annually from 1960, and the current (2003) annual publication from the African Development Bank entitled *Selected Statistics on African Countries* which gives ODA data for each country starting from 1980. Each source provides different ODA figures for each year, and in some cases the differences are significant. For example, external assistance to Ethiopia in 1997 was 605 million USD according to UNDP, 116 million according to OECD, and 578 million according to the ADB. In general, the figures from UNDP are lower than those from the other two. We have chosen the UNDP data for all the years shown below not because we think UNDP is more accurate than the others but because it is the data used by donors in the country and the Ethiopian government as well.

Secondly, we should note that the level of assistance to the country is very low compared to many other African countries. On average, the country receives 16 USD per capita (and the trend is downwards), but the comparable average for Sub-Saharan African countries is 32 USD. On the other hand, aid finances between 35 to 37 percent of the country's total public expenditure (UNDP 2001).

The ODA data provided below are grouped into two periods, 1991 to 1996 (Table 1.2a), and 1997 to 2003 (Table 1.2b). The figures in the first Table are simple aggregates while those in the second are further broken down into aid sources and types of assistance. We were unable to find figures showing breakdowns for the first period. The two Tables and Table 1.3 below present the flow of assistance to the country since the present government came to power.

Table 1.2a **Total ODA to Ethiopia 1991 to 1996 (in Million USD)**

1991	1992	1993	1994	1995	1996
1001.1	1089.5	1070.3	881.1	816.1	727.2

Source: www.undp.org; UNDP 2001 gives 756.8 million for 1996

Table 1.2b **ODA to Ethiopia 1997 to 2003**
(in million USD)

Year	Total ODA	ODA in form of Loan	ODA in form of Grants		
			Total Grants	Grants to Humanitarian /Relief	Grants to Normal Socio-Economic Sectors
1997	605	114	491	181	310
1998	675	149	526	152	374
1999	730	202	528	232	296
2000	925	142	783	448	335
2001	1083	532	551	293	258
Average 1997 to 2001	**804**	**228**	**576**	**261**	**315**
2002*	1448	656	792	383	409
2003**	1584	713	871	201	670

Source: UNDP 2003a. *Note*: *2002 figures are estimates; ** 2003 figures are projections.

As the first Table shows, international assistance peaked in the early years of the present government but declined gradually from the mid-1990s. The large volume of assistance for the period until 1995 was in part to cover the cost of reconstruction after the war, to help the government demobilize the large number of Derg soldiers, to support returning refugees, and to avert serious food crises. The government's attempt to bring about a restoration of peace and stability was assisted considerably by safety net programs to the poor and to the large number of displaced and unemployed people in the country in this period. In the second period, as shown in Table 1.2b, assistance increased in magnitude from 0.6 billion USD in 1997 to 1.0 billion in 2001, and is expected to grow to a projected 1.6 billion in 2003. Actual ODA disbursement for the period 1997-2001 averaged 804 million USD. In terms of make-up, there is a clear trend that humanitarian and relief assistance is absorbing an increasing share of ODA. In the first five years, on average this category of ODA consumed 32.4 percent of total assistance. In 2000, humanitarian/relief assistance amounted to almost half of all aid. The figures for 2002 and 2003 show a declining trend, however, these estimates were made before the current massive food crisis was anticipated. Another point to note is that the grants portion of ODA is quite high and is expected to remain about 55 percent of the total aid in 2003. It can also be noted that the loan portion of ODA has jumped from 19 percent in 1997 to 45 percent in 2003.

Table 1.3 and Figure 1.1 below show ODA trends over the same period by source. Except in the year 2000, multilateral assistance was much higher than bilateral assistance, and the two international financial institutions, in particular the World Bank, provided an increasing share of the total ODA. Bilateral assistance peaked in 2000 to reach 575 million USD and has declined since then. At the outbreak of the Ethio-Eritrean war, many donors suspended assistance, and the notable decline in bilateral assistance shown in 1999 is a result of this measure, though it appears that this decline was made up by increased assistance by multilateral donors. Aid was resumed in 2000 with the signing of the peace accords, and both bilateral and multilateral assistance helped the government in its recovery, demobilization and reintegration programs. The U.S. remains the largest bilateral donor, disbursing on average 39 percent of total bilateral assistance for the period. It is followed by Japan, a distant second with 11 percent of the total and Germany third with 6 percent. Of the total multilateral assistance, the World Bank contributed (on average) 40 percent, donors in the UN system (FAO, UNDP, UNHCR, UNICEF, etc.) 31 percent, the EU 14 percent and the African Development Bank 10 percent.

Table 1.3: **ODA Trends by Source 1997 to 2003**
(in million USD)

Donor	1997	1998	1999	2000	2001	2002	2003	Average 1997 to 2001
ODA	605	675	730	925	1083	1448	1584	804
Bilateral	263	303	247	575	402	345	390	358
Multilateral	342	372	483	350	681	1103	1194	446
UN System (FAO, UNDP, UNHCR, etc)	149	130	213	203	148	274	305	169
WB and IMF	58	72	149	105	322	583	662	141
Non-UN system	134	148	121	42	211	246	227	131

Source: UNDP 2003a

Figure 1.1 Average Share of ODA By Ten Largest Bilateral Donors, 1997 to 2003

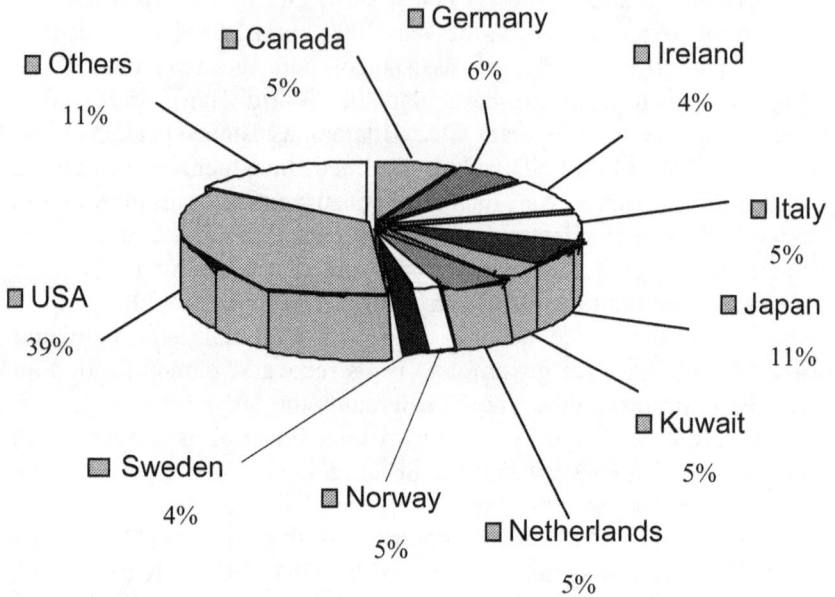

Germany
Canada 6%
Others 5%
11%
Ireland
4%

Italy
5%

USA
39%
Japan
11%

Kuwait
5%

Sweden
4%
Norway
5%
Netherlands
5%

Source: UNDP 2003a

The development sectors that have benefited from international assistance were transport, agriculture and the social service sector (health and education). At the macro level, ODA amounted to, on the average, 13 percent of GDP over the period 1997-2001, and ODA flows are growing at a faster rate than GDP growth, which averaged about 5.6 percent in the same period. Such a high level of assistance relative to GDP reflects the high level of humanitarian aid which has a limited impact on economic growth.

b. Humanitarian/Relief Assistance

The bulk of the humanitarian/relief assistance has been channeled to the country in the form of food aid. Food crisis, including famine, has been a recurrent tragedy in Ethiopia during much of the twentieth century, bringing suffering and death to innumerable peasant families and helping to prepare the ground for the collapse of both the Imperial and Derg regimes. The virulent famines of the 1960s, 1970s, and 1980s brought devastation to a wide section of the rural population in many parts of the country. More recently, the food shortages of 1994,

16

and the famine of 1999/2000 caused large-scale deprivation and loss of human lives and livestock, putting enormous pressure on the present government. Behind these publicized tragedies are a large number of localized disasters which do not often attract media or donor attention, but whose impact on the population concerned is just as devastating. There is sufficient evidence that dearth and starvation have deep-rooted structural causes and are not a product of temporary social or environmental shocks. We also know that food shortages and famines have occurred with greater frequency since the 1960s than at any time before[2]. This must be seen against a background of growing poverty on the one hand and declining agricultural performance on the other over last five decades.

The vulnerable population, that is people who are supported by food aid, has been growing rapidly in the last five decades, though we have reliable statistical evidence for the 1980s and 1990s only. In the decade between 1980 and 1989, the vulnerable population averaged 4.2 million per year; in the period 1992-2001, the comparable figure was 5.3 million. In 1993, the third year of the new government, 7.6. million peasants (or 17 percent of the rural population) were facing acute food shortages; in 1994, the figure was 6.7 million (or 15 percent). In both decades, 11 percent of the rural population was vulnerable annually. At present, the government has formally declared that 14 million people are vulnerable across the whole of the country.

The flow of food aid into the country in the last three decades is also a good indication of the growing inability of the agricultural economy to feed the peasant population. According to government figures, the amount of food aid distributed in the country in the last three decades has increased dramatically. In the decade of the 1970s, a total of 688,500 metric tons (mt) of food aid was distributed; on the average, this was 76,500 mt per year. In the 1980s, the food aid flow had jumped to 5.1 million mt, and the annual average was 512,400 mt. In the period 1991 to 2000, the total and annual average figures were 8.0 million and 798,800 mt respectively. The evidence shows that between 20 to 25 percent of the food consumed in the rural areas in the 1990s was made up of food aid. The European Union and USAID, followed a distant third by Canada, are the largest donors of food aid to the country (not counting WFP as a donor). These three donors provide about 50 percent of the food delivered to the country in any one year (WFP website).

---

[2] For the evidence for the discussion on the frequency of famine and dearth see Dessalegn 1994. The figures regarding vulnerability and the flow of food aid come from CSA and DPPC for which see Dessalegn 2003a.

c. Assistance to Democratization and Governance

A brief discussion of assistance to governance and democratization is now in order. It has been difficult to get aggregate figures on the subject; we have searched all data sources on ODA and external assistance but none include figures on this subject. Assistance provided in this sector by donors is not shown in either UNDP's, OECD's or ADB's documents cited above. The problem is further complicated by the fact that assistance to programs in this sector is frequently channeled through NGOs or civil society organizations in general, and it is not often easy to distinguish what has gone to governance programs and what to non-governance programs.

It should be pointed out, however, that many of the major bilateral and multilateral donors have provided support to governance and democratization programs of one sort or another. Among the bilateral donors one may cite the U.S., Norway, Sweden, Netherlands, Canada, Germany, Italy and U.K.[3] The programs commonly funded may be grouped into five broad categories: support to the electoral process; improvements in the justice and court systems; capacity building for Parliament; support to civil society and to the media. In a number of cases, support to elections has meant capacity building for the National Election Board (NEB), campaign finance channeled through UNDP and NEB, and funds to civil society groups to run civic or voter educations programs.

The available evidence suggests that overall such assistance makes up a small percentage of donors' total assistance to the country. There is also reason to suspect that some of the major donors have cut down on governance assistance for a variety of reasons[4]. There is a shift of emphasis from democratization and governance to socio-economic and humanitarian assistance, and the shift, spearheaded by the U.S., has been justified on the grounds that economic growth must be a priority and that support to the democratic process will be made if it contributes to development, and in particular to the poverty reduction. Canadian assistance, for example, puts heavy emphasis on supporting the government's poverty reduction program, entitled SDPRP and initiated in 2002. One suspects also that donors welcome the shift because support to democratization is bound to be

---

[3] The AIDA website's list of donors for civil society and governance programs to Ethiopia does not include multilateral donors The list gives prominence mainly to Norway, Sweden, Netherlands; the U.S. and U.K are cited a few times, but Germany and Canada are hardly mentioned.

[4] See for example USAID briefing handouts, Canadian Embassy 2003, 2004.

contentious since invariably there are bound to be failings in human rights and the electoral process which may lead to conflict or diplomatic standoff between donors and the government. While figures are not available, we have been informed that USAID's .governance fund has been decreasing in the last few years not just for Ethiopia but worldwide. The Governance Department of USAID-Ethiopia was merged with another Department and its main officer's contract was not renewed because of budget cuts[5]. The Agency's recent briefings indicate that USAID has been running down its democratic and governance program and shifting the emphasis of its country assistance to other sectors, in particular to what it calls human resource development, i.e. education and health (USAID Ethiopia website)

However, some donors continue to provide strong support to human rights and governance programs, the bulk of which is channeled through civil society institutions. A few examples may be cited here. Norway's assistance to good governance and democratization programs has been robust and has steadily increased over the years. More than one-third of Norway's bilateral assistance to Ethiopia in 2002, for example, went to support the work being done by civil society in the country, in particular in the areas of human rights, good governance and democracy. According to the Norwegian Ambassador in Addis Ababa, if the funds provided by Norway from its other budget posts are added up together, civil society receives "more bilateral and humanitarian aid from the Norwegian Government than the total amount channeled to the Government of Ethiopia and the multilateral system" (Norwegian Embassy 2003).

Similarly, Canada has maintained a strong support program to democratization and governance; indeed, since the end of the 1990s it has pledged more money for this sector than before although the emphasis now is on assistance to democratic programs that directly support development. Canada's aid agency, CIDA, has identified Ethiopia, along with six other developing countries, as the focal point of its development assistance. Its support to improved governance has been running since 1994, and between that year and 2000 it spent over 2.4 million USD on various projects focusing on legal and justice reform and capacity building (Canadian Embassy 2003). On the other hand, the European Commission, which had not had any serious programs on governance and democratization until the Cotonu Agreement of 2000 (see below), has now earmarked a budget of 25

---

[5] Oral information by Polhemus. See also USAID briefing handouts.

million Euros for such programs for this country for the years 2002-2007 (interview with Vetter). At the time of our interview, there were no programs that were being funded but there were several in the pipeline with implementation planned to start in 2004.

In conclusion, three important points may be drawn from the discussion on international assistance presented above. First, the Ethiopian government is heavily dependent on international donors without which it cannot undertake development programs, feed its population, or even run its own administrative machinery. According to the World Bank (2003), for example, aid finances about 37 percent of the government's public expenditure. Secondly, this dependence is exacerbated due to the fact that a high and growing proportion of international assistance goes to humanitarian/relief programs, meaning essentially to feed the country's increasingly hungry population; this assistance does not contribute to economic development. Finally, the donors which should have considerable leverage over the government due to their significant contributions to both development and humanitarian assistance are the U.S., the World Bank, the European Commission, and the African Development Bank group. While Japan with 11 percent, and Germany with 6 percent of total ODA may command some attention from the government, Canada and three European countries (including the Netherlands) with 5 percent each, and a number of UN agencies (UNICEF, UNDP, UNHCR) with similar contributions compete for influence on the government. Putting it in realistic terms, it may be argued that out of a total of some 45 donor countries, only a handful, perhaps not more than five, provide assistance significant enough to exercise leverage over the government if they wish to do so.

5. Methodology

This study is based on information, observations and insights, and statistical material gathered from a wide range of sources. The following is a brief discussion of these.

Interviews

We conducted a large number of interviews with a) government officials; b) officials from a select number of donor agencies; c) persons in responsible positions in a number of civil society organizations on the one hand and newspaper editors, publishers, as well as government and independent media specialists on the other.

20

The term 'civil society organizations' in this country refers to non-government groups that are involved in human rights, advocacy, civic education, and in general, non-service delivery activities. Those whose activities are primarily service delivery and emergency relief are referred to as NGOs (see Hyden 1997 for the debate).

The government officials we interviewed included the head of the country's National Election Board, officials at the Ministry of Information, officials of the Ethics and Anti-corruption Commission and an official from the Mass Media Training Institute.

The donor agencies we selected were USAID, EC, the Netherlands Embassy, Canadian CIDA, and the British DFID. Later, we obtained information from the Norwegian Embassy. There are some fifty or so bilateral and multilateral donor agencies in the country each one of which has provided assistance of one kind or another to the government in the last ten years. The five we decided to select for the study have invested, relatively speaking, significant resources in the country's democratization effort in the last ten years.

Arranging interviews or gathering information from donors is an immensely difficult task. First, there is high staff turnover among embassies and aid agencies. Officials' term of duty is usually three years, at the end of which they are either transferred elsewhere or in some cases leave the diplomatic service. The new officials that replace them lack the experience, and/or do not have ready access to the information that we were seeking. On a number of occasions, information is not found in readily accessible form, or does not exist altogether. It is interesting to note that we found government institutions had a better system of information management and were better able to provide information than many of the donor agencies we approached. The institutional memory of the agencies in question leaves a lot to be desired. Moreover, since what we were looking for was not only hard information but also observations, comments and insights, which can only come with experience in the job, the new officials were unable to be of much help. Finally, since many of the officials we spoke to were diplomatic staff and some of the answers we got were either not candid or were carefully couched in diplomatic language in which the substance was lost.

Documents
We gathered a large body of documentary evidence from government agencies, the donor community, civil society organizations, and the media. Many of these records are unpublished internal documents,

21

occasionally merely computer print-outs. We have deposited many of the published and unpublished material at the FSS library.

Newspapers
We selected five independent and two government newspapers for closer examination. We read these papers on a regular basis to examine their content, concerns and management. Both authors are also familiar with many of the other papers published in the country, including the English language ones, as well as the broadcast media discussed in the report.

Published Material
We have made use of relevant published material for the discussion in each of the chapters. The sources in question consist of both primary material (ie., government and donor publications), as well as secondary materials- ie., books, monographs, articles, and occasionally, source material downloaded from the internet. The works also include papers, articles and monographs published by the present authors.

Authors' Personal Experience
The personal experience of the authors themselves has been a valuable input. The two authors were active observers and participants of the developments that are discussed in this study, and have done considerable research on subjects relevant to the discussion at hand.

6. Outline of the Study

The discussion that follows has four parts. Chapter II will focus on the electoral context and international assistance to the country's major elections. There have been three major national and regional elections since the new government came to power. Each of the elections will be discussed from the point of view of management and participation on the one hand and the contributions of international assistance to the success or failure of the electoral process. Chapter III is on human rights and human rights organizations, and the impact of international assistance in this sector. Chapter IV is on international assistance and the media. Many donors have provided support of one sort or another to the country's fledgling private press. There has not been much support to the government media and hence this subject has not been discussed at length though there are passing comments and references to it. The country boasts over seventy newspaper and news magazines and the fact that such large numbers are being published, while a welcome change from the past, has nevertheless created problems for the press itself. We shall discuss the nature of the assistance provided and the impact it has had on the media. We present in Chapter V our overall conclusions based on our findings and the insights we have gained in the course of the study.

II. INTERNATIONAL ELECTORAL ASSISTANCE

1. Introduction

Elections in post-insurrection states have often been used to bring about peace and stability to once strife-torn societies. The agreement of conflicting parties to cease   hostilities and conduct dialogue is an essential precondition for elections to be successful in ending years of political turmoil. Once peace reigns, the verdict of the people as expressed in free and fair elections will serve as a basis for sharing power and constituting a transitional administration that will be a precursor to a popularly elected permanent government. Often, it is such a government that is expected to bring about lasting peace and reconciliation.   However, the experiences of many post-conflict states suggest that interim elections are not a smooth ride and have not always led to successful outcomes because of continuing violence and rebuttal by any one of the parties to abide by the choice of the electorate.

Time and again, the international community has intervened and supported elections to bring about peace and order in states shattered by many years of civil war. According to Kumar and Ottaway (1998), the international community has often provided financial, technical and political assistance to organize elections in post-conflict states. These forms of assistance have proved valuable in conducting elections that lead conflict-ridden nations towards democracy and political stability. Public opinion in donor countries supports such initiatives because the alternative to inaction is continuous political and economic turmoil in such states and untold suffering for their peoples. For obvious reasons, the Western public can ill-afford to sit back and watch indifferently an unfolding crisis of immense proportions. Simply put, the advantages of electoral assistance in ending incessant instability and war cannot be overemphasized, and over the past few years there have been tremendous efforts to make such assistance more effective in steering crisis-ridden states along the path towards permanent peace and stability.

Ethiopia has conducted a number of elections since 1991, the last one being in 2000, and has received substantial international electoral assistance for conducting these elections. The driving force behind much of the bilateral and multi-lateral electoral assistance has been the desire to pull the country out of many years of war-torn politics and create a stable and peaceful nation-state that would be inclusive of all opposition groups that fought against the Derg's dictatorial military regime (Harbeson 1998; Kassahun 2003).

2. Electoral Context

Ethiopia has had an election record dating back to the time of the Imperial era. The first electoral law in the country's history was promulgated in the 1950s and consisted of many articles on prohibited acts and unfair practices during public elections. Later, this law was amended in 1969 and the Central Election Board was created under the Ministry of Interior to conduct elections throughout the empire. It contained provisions on voter rights and obligations, registration and qualifications of candidates, number of constituencies, proper conduct of elections, counting of ballots and announcement of results. The Derg regime, which succeeded the Imperial Government, also adopted a similar system of electoral structure, including a national electoral board and a set of penal code provisions against offences during public elections.

At present, Ethiopia has a bi-cameral Parliament consisting of a House of Peoples Representatives (HPR) and a House of Federation (HoF). According to the 1995 Federal Constitution, both Houses are elected for a 5-year term. The HPR has 550 seats, acts as the lower House of Parliament and is the main organ that makes laws and approves major policies of the government. The HoF is a de facto Upper House composed of representatives of nations, nationalities and peoples of the Federal Republic of Ethiopia. According to the Constitution, this house consists of at least one member from each nation and nationality and one additional representative for each one million population of the nationality or nation. Although constitutionally important as a representative body, the HoF does not have formal law making powers but decides on issues relating to the rights of nations and nationalities to self-determination, including secession. Its other main responsibility is to provide interpretations on constitutional issues.

Members to the House of Representatives are elected on the basis of a plurality of votes cast in single member constituencies. Under this system, the candidate who receives the highest number of votes is declared the winner and others are dropped regardless of the number of votes cast in their favor. This electoral practice precludes the representation of candidates having alternative programs and views other than the winning candidate with the highest number of votes. In electoral systems that do not provide for a level playing field, such as Ethiopia's current system, this practice can give undue advantage to the party in power especially when the government has complete control over the mass media and other state resources and uses the same to influence the outcome of the elections in its favor.

In several discussions with the authors, most opposition parties in Ethiopia have severely criticized the current single member constituency system as being undemocratic and favoring the ruling party. They have repeatedly called for changes to the constitution to allow for 'proportional representation'[6]. Proportional representation makes it possible for different political forces to share parliamentary seats in proportion to their electoral strength. In principle, no political force or part of public opinion retains a monopoly; at the same time, none is excluded from representation. Hence, the system's main virtue is said to be justice. Another advantage of this system is that voting takes place in a single round and the 'politicking and bickering', which often takes place in systems practicing a second round, is avoided (IPU 1993).

Ethiopia has a parliamentary form of government in which the House of Peoples Representatives (HPR) elects the Prime Minister. There is a State President who serves for a six-year term but his/her role and functions are largely ceremonial. As the leader of the party with the largest number of seats in parliament, the Prime Minister is the chief executive officer and wields tremendous power in the running of the country as well as in his relation with the legislature and the judiciary. He/she has the authority to dissolve the HPR but is required to call elections within six months of the latter's dissolution. One-party executive dominance is a typical feature of the Ethiopian government and this has meant a weak system of checks and balances among the three organs of government.

As indicated elsewhere in this report, Ethiopia's electoral experience dates back to the Imperial era. Through Proclamation No. 158 of 1957, the Imperial Government defined a series of 'offenses against public elections and voting' and corresponding punishments. Later, Proclamation No. 28 of 1969 was issued dealing with 'Parliament and Elections'. The law established the country's first

---

[6] Interview with Ledetu Ayalew, Secretary-General, Ethiopian Democratic Party (EDP)

electoral board, defined its powers and duties and set out registration and voting principles and procedures. In spite of its leftist ideological rhetoric, the Derg conducted elections by following similar practices and principles enshrined in the Imperial legislation. There was little competition in elections under the monarchy because the overwhelming majority of parliamentary candidates were supporters of the Imperial regime. Under the Derg, only candidates of the sole ruling party run for parliamentary seats. As a result, elections were neither free nor competitive under the two regimes. Further, both the Imperial regime and its successor, the Derg military dictatorship, did not allow international monitoring and supervision of national elections. EPRDF's inclination to allow election monitoring and supervision clearly sets it apart from its predecessors.

3. Post-Conflict Elections

Upon coming to power in 1991, EPRDF made a public commitment to democracy, national reconciliation and a broad-based government that will be inclusive of all vying groups that fought against the Derg regime. Subsequently, it has already carried out 4 major elections: the 1992 interim elections; 1995 national parliamentary elections; the 1995 constituent assembly elections and the 2000 national assembly elections. All are intended to consolidate peace and order throughout the country, and create a proper climate for economic reconstruction and development. At present, the country is bracing itself for another round of nation-wide parliamentary elections in 2005. It is necessary to review the purposes and outcomes of these elections to provide a proper scene for assessing their contribution to peaceful transition and the prospects for democracy in post-Derg Ethiopia.

a. The 1992 Interim Elections

Following the ousting of the Derg regime by the Ethiopian Peoples Revolutionary Democratic Forces (EPRDF) in 1991, the country conducted its first interim national elections that led to the establishment of the Transitional Government of Ethiopia (TGE) in 1992. The TGE was set up in the wake of the London and Addis Ababa peace conferences and was entrusted with the task of administering the country on a provisional basis under a transitional charter. Under the charter, the TGE was committed to conduct regional and local elections within three months of its establishment, drafting a new constitution, which required elections for a constituent assembly and holding national elections under the new constitution within two-and-half years.

The EPRDF conducted the 1992 elections at national, regional and woreda levels to establish a Transitional Government that could fill the gap created by Derg's departure. The elections took place in about 450 of the 600 woredas. These were hastily prepared and quite a number of ethnic-based liberation groups that fought the Derg regime participated. As Ethiopia's first post-Derg elections, the elections were characterized by chaos and poor organization of the electoral process. Election irregularities were widely reported raising serious concerns about the legitimacy of the outcome as being the true wish of the people. More than any thing else, the EPRDF affiliated parties manipulated the elections in most of the constituencies to insure complete victory (Vestal, 2000; NDI, 1992).

The attempt to establish a broad-based government following the 1992 elections was unsuccessful because major political and ethnic groups boycotted the elections on grounds of 'unfair and unequal conditions' for participation set out by the dominant EPRDF coalition (Pausewang and Tronvoll 2000).[7] Although controversial, however, these elections were important in setting the stage for the division of the country into ethnic regions controlled by parties closely affiliated to the EPRDF. The Amhara National Democratic Movement (ANDM), the Tigrean Peoples' Liberation Front (TPLF), the Oromo Peoples Democratic Movement (OPDM) and the South Ethiopia Peoples' Democratic Coalition (SEPDC) constitute the core parties of the EPRDF. About 45 other smaller predominantly ethnic parties are supported by and work with the EPRDF coalition but are not member organizations of the Front. Over the years, ethhnic parties closely allied with the EPRDF emerged as single ruling parties in their respective regions with little or no challenge from opposition parties. This eventually helped the EPRDF to solidify its control over the different regions because the parties affiliated with the coalition continued to provide the bedrock for its power.

---

[7] One of the major groups which boycotted these elections was the Oromo Liberation Front (OLF).

b. The 1995 Constituent Assembly Elections

The EPRDF conducted the 1995 Constituent Assembly Elections following the appointment of a constitution drafting commission by the Council of Representatives of the Transitional Government. This commission was entrusted with the task of preparing a draft constitution that was to be adopted by an elected assembly. The credibility of the commission was seriously questioned by opposition groups and political observers as the positions of chairmanship, vice-chairmanship and secretary were held by members of the EPRDF (Kassahun, 2003). The opposition and critics of the government saw it as a move by the EPRDF to pre-empt any alternative vision for the future of the Ethiopian state and entrench the ruling party in power.

The 1995 constituent assembly elections resulted in the adoption of a Constitution that established a federal state structure composed of quasi-sovereign ethnic-based Regional states. The Constitution devolved considerable powers and authority to the regions and transformed Ethiopia from one of a highly centralized unitary government to a decentralized federal state. While much of this exercise was important to the extent that it aided the country's peaceful transition, the inclusion of the controversial Article 39 of the Constitution, which sanctions secession for any nationality or ethnic group, has to this day continued to be a source of acrimony among groups with different visions for the future of the Ethiopian state.

Table 2.1 **Constituent Assembly Election Results – 1995**

No.	Region	Estimated eligible voters	Registered voters	Actual Votes cast	Number of Wining candidates
1.	Tigray	1,549,192	1,226,208	1,146,510	37
2.	Afar	355,196	358,170	291,764	8
3.	Amhara	6,392,052	3,916,118	3,517,781	137
4.	Oromiya	8,072,722	5,197,913	4,444,640	177
5.	Somale	2,399,984	1,607,532	1,396,933	23
6.	SNNPR	4,810,319	3,590,440	3,277,368	123
7.	Gambella	53,784	49,316	26,085	3
8.	Harari	80,750	35,304	31,212	3
9.	Dire Dawa	184,221	66,702	40,794	2
10.	Addis Ababa	1,128,781	593,946	398,044	23
	TOTAL	25,359,550	16,778,620	14,697,992	536

Source: National Election Board, Report to the House of Representatives, Addis Ababa, 1997

Voter turnout for the 1995 elections was low compared to earlier elections. According to data obtained from NEB, out of more than 25 million eligible voters, only about 15 million or only 60 per cent of the eligible electorate actually voted. As in the 1995 national elections to the House of Representatives, however, EPRDF had again a landslide victory winning 460 (90 %) of the total 510 organized constituencies. This assured EPRDF an unquestionable hegemony in shaping the form and content of Ethiopia's post-Derg Constitution; and set the stage for legitimizing two singularly important and core agendas of the dominant EPRDF for the future Ethiopian state ---the division of the country along ethno-linguistic lines and constitutionally enshrined right of any nation or nationality to secede from the federation.

c. *The 1995 First National Assembly Elections*

After nearly 4 years in power as a transitional authority, the EPRDF ruling group conducted the 1995 parliamentary elections to provide for a permanent government. These were largely peaceful and took place in a climate of relative political calm and order throughout much of the country. Nevertheless, many opposition groups and independent candidates boycotted the elections; and allegations of intimidation, imprisonment and voting irregularities were widely reported (Tronvoll and Aadland 1995; Polhemus 2002). In addition, the elections had other shortcomings, including insufficient civic education, apathy among the voting public especially among the rural peasantry and the absence of a strong and united opposition that could provide an alternative (Pausewang and Tronvoll 2000). Despite the inadequacies, however, the EPRDF had a landslide victory and managed to assert complete control of the executive and the legislature.

Table 2.2 **House of Representatives National Election Results—1995**

No.	Region	Registered voters	Actual votes cast	Number of winning candidates	
				M	F
1.	Tigray	1,364,087	1,341,850	36	2
1.	Afar	574,616	503,483	8	--
3.	Amhara	5,447,236	5,268,501	137	1
4.	Oromyia	6,191,826	5,855,598	174	3
5.	Somale	2,294,497	2,086,869	23	----
6.	Benishangul-Gumuz	213,665	195,487	9	-----
7.	SNNPR	4,473,679	4,204,693	123	----
8.	Gambella	52,487	32,228	3	------
9.	Harari	60,357	52,412	2	------
10.	Dire Dawa	1,005,51	82,378	2	------
11.	Addis Ababa	564,378	445,058	19	4
	Total	21,337,379	19,986,179	536	10

Source: National Election Board, Report to the House of Representatives,
　　　Addis Ababa, 1997.

When the results of the 1995 national elections were announced by the National Election Board, EPRDF scored an overwhelming victory winning 89 per cent (491 out of the 546 seats) of the parliamentary seats. Political groups not directly allied with the EPRDF and independent candidates won 19 per cent, out of which more than 55 per cent was filled by region-based ethnic parties which were not members of the ruling coalition but were under the direct tutelage of the EPRDF, such as the Somali Democratic League and the Benishangul People's Unity Party.

d. *The 2000 National Elections*

After its first 5-year term expired as a permanent government, EPRDF conducted the 2000 national, regional and woreda elections to provide a second term for itself. The elections took place at a time when relative peace and stability have reigned over much of the country. It was also a period when law and order was much improved throughout the country in sharp contrast to the in 1992 and

1995 elections when the EPRDF had not yet firmly established state authority throughout the nation. Nevertheless, it was also a time when the general public has not yet come to grips with the disastrous consequences of the 1998 Ethio-Eritrean border war and the ensuing fragile ceasefire. In 2000, the Government signed the Algiers Peace Agreement immediately before the elections. Although the Government scored a landslide victory in the polls, it is difficult to determine the extent to which the signing of the Peace Agreement might have helped its cause in influencing the outcome.

Table 2.3 **National Election Results for the House of Representatives---2000**[8]

No.	Region	Number of registered voters	Number of actual votes cast	Voter turnout (%age)
1.	Tigray	1,391,575	1,338,197	96.1
2.	Afar	495,181	328,908	94.9
3.	Amhara	5,333,079	5,293,553	99.2
4.	Oromiya	7,006,783	6,396,025	89
5	Benishangul-Gumuz	205,489	172,865	84
6.	SNNPR	4,630.308	4,043,351	86.4
7.	Gambella	94,565	93,563	98.9
8.	Harari	56,295	56,066	99.5
9.	Dire Dawa	112,307	74,484	66.3
10.	Addis Ababa	849,510	664,759	78.2
	Total	20,354,156	18,659,481	91.6

Source: NEB, Addis Ababa, 2001

The 2000 elections provided legitimacy to the EPRDF for a second term and were handsomely won by the ruling party. As Table 2.4 below indicates, a total of 1156 candidates competed at the national level. There were 412 independent candidates and 744 candidates were put up by about 50 political parties that participated in the competition.

---

[8] Election results in the Somale Region are not included in the table.

32

Table 2.4 **Number of Candidates in the 2000 Elections**

No.	Description	Number of Candidates	%
1.	Number of EPRDF and other party candidates	744	64
2.	Number of independent candidates	412	36
3.	Total number of candidates	1156	100

Source: Compiled by the Authors and Berhanu and Meleskachew 2001.

There were a total 547 parliamentary seats in the 2000 elections. Out of these, 263 or about 48.1 % were uncontested, i.e. only one candidate ran unopposed often from the ruling party, and thus went automatically to the ruling EPRDF. As shown in the Table 2.5, by winning 481 (88 percent) out of the 547 parliamentary seats, The EPRDF assured an overwhelming victory for itself.

Table 2.5 **Number of Parliamentary Seats in the 2000 Elections**

No.	Description	Number of Seats	%
1.	Number of parliamentary seats won by EPRDF affiliate parties and uncontested seats	481	87.9
2.	Number of parliamentary seats won by the opposition	53	9.6
3.	Number of Independent seats	13	2.3
4.	Total number of parliamentary seats	547	100

Source: Compiled by the Authors and Berhanu and Meleskachew 2001.

Of all the national elections that the EPRDF conducted in its nearly ten years of rule, the 2000 national elections were by far significant, better organized and showed a relative degree of competitiveness especially in the Southern Region and some urban areas like Addis Ababa and Dire Dawa. There was much more spirited public discussion of issues among candidates representing different parties, and the people followed many of these elections with a great deal of interest. More important, the government allowed limited access to the state controlled media and airtime for campaigning by opposition and independent candidates. Still, however, the electronic media was

33

largely dominated by politicians from the ruling party as can be evidenced by the fact provided in Table 2.6 below.

Table 2.6 Estimated Use of Free Air Time by Parties and Government Officials in the 2000 Elections (in minutes)

No.	Organization/Politician	Radio	Television
1.	AAPO - Opposition	15	15
2.	EDP - Opposition	15	15
3.	EPRDF - Ruling Party	57	57
4.	Meles Zenawi - Prime Minister	60	60
5.	Ali Abdo --------Ruling Party	30	30
6.	Addisu Legesse - " "	45	45
7.	Abate Kisho - " "	42	42
8.	Kuma Demeksa " "	40	40
9	Total	304	304

Source: Berhanu and Meleskachew 2001

The airtime offered to pro-government and opposition candidates was highly skewed in favor of the former. As can be observed in the Table above, a total of 304 minutes of airtime was used by different politicians out of which the opposition used only 30 minutes for radio and TV each, and this represented about 10 per cent of the total airtime. In contrast, politicians and officials of the ruling party used nearly 90 per cent of the airtime indicating a preponderant use of the electronic media by the party that controlled the state. This definitely gave undue advantage to the ruling party in introducing its programs and plans to the electorate. The role of the electronic media, particularly radio broadcasting, is critical in a country like Ethiopia where print media reach only a small proportion of the people. Hence, it is absolutely necessary to provide fair access to all the parties to guarantee a level playing field for competition during elections.

Elections during the Imperial and Derg eras were neither democratic nor free. In both regimes, they were tightly controlled from above and largely ceremonial activities, which the people had to carry out as an expression of their obedience to the authority of the state. The public line up and cast their ballots because failure to do so can bring the wrath of the government (Pausewang, Tronvoll

& Aalen, 2002). Under the monarchy, there were no political parties and candidates had to possess immovable property; these conditions could hardly qualify the electoral process as democratic. Under the Derg, people could vote only for candidates of the regime's Marxist-Leninist Party masquerading as the Workers Party of Ethiopia (WPE). Since the elections were neither competitive nor open under the two defunct regimes, only official candidates won and often with a landslide victory. This reality is reflected in Table 2.1. It can be observed that the outcome of elections under the EPRDF reflect an extremely interesting resemblance to the two preceding regimes despite formal claims by the present government of having allowed multi-party politics.

Table 2.7 **Outcomes of Elections under the Three Regimes**

No.	Regime	Regime Characteristics	Election outcomes
1.	Imperial Regime	No parties Allowed	99% all regime candidates won
2.	Derg Regime	Single ruling party	99% victory - all regime candidates
3.	EPRDF Regime	Multi-party	95% victory for ruling party

Source: Compiled by the authors

The table shows that despite differences in regime characteristics, all the three regimes invariably won elections with a landslide victory and the ruling group held or continues to hold power unchallenged. However, it is important to note that there are also important differences among the three regimes. For example, the Imperial and Derg governments never allowed the existence of a free press and freedom of association. Neither did they allow international supervision and monitoring of elections. In contrast, there is a struggling free print media under the EPRDF and the current government has, albeit reluctantly, allowed international and domestic elections monitors to observe elections in the country. In addition, unheard of under its predecessors, the present regime has to its credit allowed the growth and functioning of independent civil society organizations, such as the Ethiopian Human Rights Council (EHRCO), which have been very active in the election process and monitoring the state of human rights in the country.

In Ethiopia, most political parties are ethnic-based and multiethnic/national parties are far too small in number. As was indicated elsewhere in this report, about 50 parties contested the last 2000 national elections and a substantial majority supported the ruling EPRDF. At present, there are a few opposition political parties but these are largely weak and ineffective in challenging the dominant EPRDF and offering alternatives to the electorate. In addition, most are urban based and thus unable to reach the larger rural constituency. They have been made less effective in part due to the heavy-handed tactics of the ruling EPRDF that includes harassment, intimidation and imprisonment of opposition party functionaries and supporters.

4. International Electoral Assistance

a. Technical and Financial Assistance for Constitutional and Legal Reforms

There was a major infusion of international electoral assistance that was given to the Ethiopian government in the early 1990s before the present NEB was formally established. This was given through the UNDP under the project title 'Assistance to the National Electoral Board of Transitional Government of Ethiopia' in May 1994 and amounted to more than 14.9 million US dollars. The UNDP grant brings the total bilateral and multi-lateral electoral assistance that Ethiopia has received between 1992-2004 to 15.5 million USD. As earlier noted, the Ethiopian government budgetary allocations to the 9 different elections conducted between 1992-2000 have run to the tune of 17.5 million USD.

The UNDP 14.9 million US dollars grant was intended to assist the NBE of the Transitional Government in preparing and carrying out the Constituent Assembly election held in 1994. In particular, the project was to assist in the planning of the elections and mobilization and coordination of external resources, and in the procurement of inputs to be financed by donor contributions through a cost sharing mechanism. It is also possible that some of the assistance could have been used in drafting the constitution and the legal provisions for elections; but, given the chaotic situation and the level of disorganization at the time, there is no evidence to assess the magnitude of the aid and its impact. More specifically, the aid was intended to be used for the provision of computer systems; wide range of civic education and polling station officer training materials, equipment and support; supplies and materials in support of voter registration, i.e. voter registration books, voter cards, pens, pencils, etc. and provision of supplies and materials in support of election-day activities.

As already discussed, the period the UNDP grant was given to conduct the constituent assembly elections in 1994 was characterized by disorganization and poor preparation of the election process. The current NEB has very little information on how the money was spent and was unable to provide any evidence that will serve as a basis to assess the impact of the assistance. In addition, no proper accounting on the use of the money could be provided by any other government agency or the UNDP. Hence, although the donation was significant and could have immensely contributed towards democratizing the electoral process, the absence of accountability in the use of resources has made it difficult to assess the full impact of the assistance.

Another factor which contributed to the relative success of the 2000 elections was the keen interest shown by the donor community and the country's major aid providers to see a democratic and competitive electoral process. The donor community in Addis Ababa set up a Donor Election Unit (DEU) to coordinate aid to the elections and political parties as well as closely follow whether the elections would be fair and free. Such a common platform helped the group to exchange information and express a common position to the Ethiopian Government if irregularities are reported in the electoral process and the outcome.

The close attention of the donor community might have helped in the creation of a better playing level field for competitive and free elections than in the past. Many embassies and bilateral and multi-lateral aid agencies based in Addis Ababa organized election monitoring missions or sent representatives to observe the election process in the different parts of the country. For example, the Embassy of the United States of America fielded 17 observers and election monitors throughout the different regions of the country and Addis Ababa. The assessments that followed were largely positive and reflected a gradual sense of optimism. According to the report of the Bureau of Democracy, Human Rights, and Labor of the U.S Department of State, "most opposition political parties competed in the May election; however, due to lack of funds and often weak organization, opposition parties contested only 20 per cent of the seats to the federal parliament" (U.S. Department of State, 2001).

b. Assistance to the National Electoral Board

Chapter 6 of the Ethiopian Federal Constitution provides for an independent National Electoral Board (NEB) to manage elections at federal, regional and local levels. The Board has seven members who are accountable to and appointed by the House of Representatives upon presentation by the Executive branch of government. It will have a Chairperson and a secretary who assumes the role of chief executive of the secretariat and is non-voting. The Constitution does not specify the term of office of the Board and the assumption is that members will continue to 'serve for good behavior'[9]. It only states that it will be composed of members designated in consideration of 'national representation, technical competence, integrity and experience'. Although set up by the Federal Government, the Constitution allows the Board to have branch offices at Regional and sub-Regional levels for organizing elections throughout the country.

The NEB has been given full and independent authority to confirm and officially announce election results as well as rectify electoral irregularities and decide on complaints submitted to it. This subsumes that it will be impartial, independent and free of any interference in carrying out its mission. However, this principle was put to a severe test in 2003 when the General Manager of the NEB was jailed for three days on charges leveled against him by the Federal Ethics and Anti-Corruption and Commission. The Commission accused him of misuse of authority and violating the constitutional right of a public employee who was arbitrarily dismissed for exposing acts of corruption in the Board. He was released after agreeing to respect the law and reinstate the suspended public servant (*Addis Zemen*, April 24, 2003; *Addis Zena*, April 22, 2003).

The order to arrest the General Manager came from a department under the executive branch of government, and this could be considered a serious threat to the independence and integrity of the National Electoral Board. Coming from the Executive branch of government, it could as well be considered as unwarranted meddling or manipulation of the Board's activities and a serious challenge to its status as an impartial body in conducting free and fair elections. Despite the serious implications that the incident signaled for the neutral status of the Board and its ability to conduct elections as an

---

[9] Interview with Assefa Birru, General Manager, National Electoral Board

impartial body, however, there is no evidence to indicate that any donor group or country providing assistance to the Government of Ethiopia took up the issue or expressed concern about the unprecedented arrest of the General Manager.

The General Manager of the NEB was sharply critical of the role of international/foreign election monitors and observers. He criticized many of them for being pre-judgmental, having ulterior agendas and bent upon fault-finding rather than providing constructive advice and suggestions to improve the electoral process. In his opinion, it is absolutely necessary to have international monitors seconded to the country well in advance of the actual elections so that they could observe the entire process from the start, including campaigning, registration, voting and counting and announcement of results. Simply put, free and fair elections do not begin and end in a polling day and as such monitors and observers should be assigned well ahead of the elections so that they will be in a position to judge the full conduct of the election process.

Furthermore, the Head of Ethiopia's NEB has reservations on direct international funding of national elections. He insisted that a government must be able to cover the full cost of elections because external funding can bring with it undue influence that can compromise the country's sovereignty and independence. In whatever form international assistance may come to advance democratic elections, it should be envisaged as solidarity or partnership in a common endeavor to conduct free and fair elections rather than being viewed as donor-recipient relationship. He also resented the fact that in many instances inexperienced recruits with little knowledge and appreciation about the history and culture of the country are often designated for monitoring elections, and this had resulted in superficial and highly impressionistic assessment of election processes and outcomes. Neutral observers with reasonable knowledge about the history and politics of the country could make significant contributions to improve the electoral system for future elections.[10]

Proponents of electoral politics argue that the cost of elections must not be expensive for parties and individual candidates because of their dampening effect on competitive politics. The experience of many African countries over the past two decades shows that the

---

[10] Interview with Assefa Birr, NEB.

costs of elections have been escalating and there is a grave danger that this might impede democracy and effective participation in election campaigns by several parties. In addition, there is also the argument that if elections become expensive, fund raising becomes the pre-occupation of politicians thereby distracting them from public policy making and their role as trustees of the public interest (Shugarman 2000; Oyugi 2003).

It is generally believed that post-conflict elections can be costly affairs for a poor nation such as Ethiopia. Often, the donor community provides assistance to offset the heavy cost of elections for poor states struggling to come out of crisis. In its post-conflict history, Ethiopia has conducted 9 national, regional and local elections under the EPRDF at a cost of nearly 17.5 million USD---a substantial amount of money for a very poor nation. This amount constituted the total budget allocated by the Government to the National Electoral Board between 1992-2000. During the same period, the country has received bilateral and multi-lateral electoral assistance to the tune of 15.5 million USD that was used to administer elections and support political parties. Table 2.8 below contains only regular budget allocations made by the Ethiopian Government to the National Electoral Board.

Table 2.8 **Cost of Elections in Ethiopia 1993/94-2001/02 (in USD[11])**

No.	Year	Area and Type of Election	Amount
1.	1995	Constituent assembly elections	5,026,394
2.	1995	First national assembly elections	469,484
3.	1996	Nationwide Woreda and Kebele elections	1,900,193
4.	1997	Afar elections	296,663
5.	1998	Debub Woredas elections	1,398,202
6.	1999	Gambella, Benishangul and nation-wide by-lections	698,338
7.	2000	Second national elections	3,370,310
8.	2000	Woreda and kebele elections in Tigray, Amhara, Oromia, Afar and Addis Ababa	3,3600,26
9.	2001	Zone, Woreda and Kebele Elections in Debub	949,426
		Total	17,469,036

Source: National Electoral Board, Addis Ababa, 2003.

---

[11] The original budget in Ethiopian Birr has been converted at the equivalent rate of 1 USD= Eth. Birr 8.52

As indicated earlier, the total budget figure in the table does not include any bilateral or multi-lateral assistance that might have come to the NEB or other civil society organizations engaged in various activities related to elections, such as voter education and monitoring elections. Available evidence suggests that international electoral assistance has been significant but, as will be argued later, its impact on democratizing the electoral process has been limited.

Cost per voter is often used as a yardstick to assess the cost of elections and make comparisons among countries. Available evidence suggests that elections can be costly affairs in some African countries. Lack of experience in administering elections, and undeveloped physical and communication infrastructure often dilapidated through many years of neglect and civil war, add to the cost of elections in many post-conflict states. Table 2.9 below presents data on election costs for some African countries. It can be observed that a comparison of election costs for selected African countries with Ethiopia shows that the cost of elections in Ethiopia has been surprisingly low given the country's enormous size and its lack of experience in running democratic elections.

Table 2.9 **Comparative Data on Cost of Elections in Selected African Countries (in U.S. Dollars)**

No.	Country	Date of Election	Total Cost	Number of voters	Total cost/ no. of voters
1.	Angola	1992	100 mills.	4.5 mills.	22
2.	Botswana	1994	1 mill.	0.37 mill.	2.7
3.	Ethiopia[12]	1995 Constituent Assembly elections	8.2 mills.	14.7 mills.	0.55
		2000 National Elections	3.5 mills.	18.7 mills	0.19
4.	Kenya	2002	45.5 mills.	5.9 mills.	7.8
4.	Lesotho	1995	6 mills.	0.83 mill.	6.9
5.	Malawi	1994	8 mills.	3.8 mills.	2.1
6.	South Africa	1994	250 mills.	22.7 mills.	11.0
7.	Tanzania	1995	Shillings 28,567,396,767	-	7.88

Source:. Fambon, 2003; NEB, 1997
Note: The figures for Ethiopia for the 1995 Constituent Assembly and 2000 National Elections are government outlay only.

---

[12] The calculation for Ethiopia was made using budgetary allocations by the Ethiopian Government.

From the preceding table, it can be observed that Ethiopia, with 0.55 and 0.19 U.S. cents per voter for the 1995 constituent assembly and 2000 national elections respectively, has conducted the least expensive elections from among the countries sampled. By all standards, Ethiopia has registered a spectacular achievement when compared with Angola's 22 and South Africa's 11 US dollars per voter. One important explanation for the low cost is the fact that the National Electoral Board in Ethiopia conducts elections by using existing government administrative structures and resources at federal, Regional, Zonal, *woreda* and *kebele* levels. In addition, the Board also deploys a huge army of government civil servants at very low rates of pay, and this keeps the cost of elections down. This practice might have enabled the country to run low-cost elections; however, serious questions can be raised as to whether the elections are going to be free and fair given the fact that they are conducted through the instrumentality of a state apparatus and public personnel both of which are under the tutelage of the ruling party and government in power.

c. Political Party Assistance

Another international electoral assistance worthy of mention is the 318,625.39 USD that was given to the NEB to be distributed to political parties during the 2000 elections. The money was distributed to 33 registered political parties through a committee chaired by the Head of the National Electoral Board. The disbursements ranged from a high of 35,798 USD, which went to the Oromo National Congress (ONC), to the smallest 586 USD, which went to the Yem Nationality Democratic Movement (NEB, 2001). A number of European countries and the UNDP contributed to the fund. Detailed information on donor contributions is provided in Table 2.10.

Table 2.10 **Assistance to Registered Political Parties for the 2000 Elections**

No.	Donor	Amount in USD
1.	UNDP	58,685.44
2.	Government of Norway	56,383.22
3.	Government of Netherlands	56,989.97
4.	Government of Sweden	58,538.58
5.	Government of Ireland	29,342.72
6.	Government of U.K.	58,685.44
	Total	318,625.39

Source: National Electoral Board, 2001.

The donation went into a provisional fund established under Proclamation No. 46/1993 at the initiative of the National Electoral Board. The objective of the fund was to provide financial assistance to legally registered political parties through the Board to enable parties to contest the general elections in a competitive manner. The support was used for communication, office space, for access to the public media and for any other measures to ensure broad participation and free and fair elections.

In general, the establishment of the provisional fund through a program of international electoral assistance was helpful in providing support to legitimate political parties and in facilitating participation in the 2000 elections. This definitely contributed to broad participation in the elections and might have aided the democratization process. Despite the positive contribution, however, there were as well some weaknesses in the distribution and utilization of the money. For example, the majority of the parties that benefited from the support have not provided complete financial reports and this has made it difficult to account for the funds in an accountable and transparent manner. Equally important, according to reports received from many political parties, the money was late in coming, and this might have reduced their effectiveness in the political competition. While there is general consensus that the support might have contributed to broad participation in the 2000 elections, none of the donor governments have insisted on reports that would show how the contributions were spent by political parties. The lack of effective follow-up and monitoring has made it difficult to assess the full impact of the international assistance on electoral politics in Ethiopia.

d. International Election Monitoring

Another factor that is significant in Ethiopia's low-cost elections is international electoral assistance that mostly comes in the form of financial, material and technical assistance. This assistance goes both to the NEB and independent civil society organizations, such as EHRCO, CRDA and others actively engaged in monitoring elections and voter education programs prior to the elections. The assistance given to the NEB is largely in the form of material and technical assistance, such as computers, vehicles and other election related assistance. In this regard, mention can be made of the roughly 300,000 US dollars that the NEB received from the United States Agency for International Development (USAID) to purchase communication and radio equipment, computers, vehicles and other accessories for the 2000 elections (NEB 2003). The executing agency for the assistance was the Washington-based International Foundation for Electoral Systems. It can be argued that this was a small portion of the cost of elections that Ethiopia incurred and its impact on democratization in this country was bound to be limited.

e. *Civic and Voter Education*

With international and bilateral electoral support, a number of civil society organizations have been active in voter and civic education programs before the 2000 elections in Ethiopia. The main ones included the Addis Ababa Chamber of Commerce (AACC), Ethiopian Women's Lawyers' Association (EWLA), the Confederation of Ethiopian Trade Unions (CETU), Eneweyay Civic and Social Education Center (ECSEC) and the Society for the Advancement of Human Rights (SAHRE). These represented a small segment of the civil organization community and were limited in outreach because they could cover only Addis Ababa, Dire Dawa and some cities in the Southern Region. In addition, many of them started their work close to the elections and as a result their impact has been limited (CLCBS 2003).

   To carry out a better coordinated program of voter and civic education, a group of six NGOs had established the Ethiopian Non-Governmental Organizations Consortium for Elections (ENCONEL)--2000 in early 1999. The objectives of the Consortium 'were to develop standard and coherent teaching materials for voters' education; to determine target areas for voters' education among the constituent NGOs in order to avoid a geographical duplication of efforts as well as to maximize the use of scarce resources; and, finally, to apply a coordinated and structured approach towards the donors in the process of equitably using the limited available resources' (CLCBS, 2003).

Voter and civic education programs prior to the 200 elections focused on human rights and the law, good governance, the Ethiopian electoral law and election processes and procedures. Some of the programs initiated by civil society organizations in Ethiopia had either targeted audiences or were intended to advance the cause of a particular constituency. For example, with assistance from FES (Friedrich Ebert Stiftung), the British Council in Addis Ababa and CIDA, EWLA's activities focused on increasing the participation of women in the elections. With assistance from the USAID, CETU arranged public forms for political parties and individuals to introduce their programs to workers. It also encouraged workers to participate actively in the national elections. Through a project known as 'Vote Addis', the Addis Ababa Chamber of Commerce (AACC) launched a campaign encouraging candidates to properly articulate the agenda of the business community to the voters. It also focused on supporting the media to cover the election in a fair and acceptable manner and serve as a bridge between candidates and voters.

5. Impact of Electoral Assistance

Bent upon improving its image as a democratic government domestically and abroad, the EPRDF regime organized a number of elections in a bid to open the country's politics to multi-party competition. However, none of the elections it conducted were judged to be neither free nor competitive because voting irregularities were widely reported and the main opposition parties boycotted the elections (AAI/NDI 1992; Aalen 2002; Pausewang, Tronvoll and Aalen 2002; Polhemus 2002). More important, the ruling party using state and bureaucratic resources under its control repeatedly gained an overwhelming victory and the people were not given real options to choose from (Abbink 2000). Hence, serious questions are being raised about prospects for democratic politics and multi-partyism in Ethiopia at least in the not-too-distant future given recent setbacks in providing a level playing field for competitive and open elections.

Compared to the Derg era, Ethiopia has enjoyed relative peace following the series of elections discussed earlier, and the international community has provided considerable reconstruction and humanitarian assistance to aid the country's peaceful transition. As in many other similar states, however, elections in Ethiopia have not achieved full reconciliation among the protagonists because some important contending groups were not included in the post-insurrection power structure (Asnake 2001). As a result, substantial anxiety still exists about the long-term stability of the political order and its inability to be inclusive of all groups.

In assessing the value and contribution of election monitoring and observation to the democratization process, diplomatic staff of different embassies and donors based in Addis Ababa expressed differing views. In informal discussions that the writers had with representatives of selected foreign embassies, it was revealed that the intention of such missions was not to influence or pressurize the Government but to see to it that elections in Ethiopia followed international standards and practices. Equally important, it can be argued that election monitoring in Ethiopia should be undertaken by external actors to see to it that the Government adheres to the principles and standards of democratic practice that it had vowed to uphold upon coming to power.

When it comes to external involvement and monitoring of elections particular mention must be made of the role of the Delegation of the European Commission in Addis Ababa, which organized an observer mission that carefully assessed Ethiopia's election in accordance with the official policy to support free and competitive elections in emerging democracies (CEC 2002).

As a typical post-conflict state, Ethiopia has received substantial international electoral assistance for the series of elections conducted between 1992-2000. Such assistance has built the institutional and logistical capacity of the National Electoral Board to administer elections. In addition, donor assistance has also been provided to strengthen civil society and human rights organizations, develop and institutionalize political parties, conduct public debates and discussions during and before elections and run voter education and training programs. However, the impact of such assistance on democratizing the electoral process has been limited.

The electoral process in Ethiopia has been consistently dominated by a single ruling party, which has failed to provide a level playing field for competitive, fair and free elections for all contestants that could provide alternative choices to the electorate. Hence, contrary to the expectations of bilateral and multi-lateral donors, Ethiopia's transition to peace and democracy has been fraught with problems because the political regime has failed to be all inclusive; and has not broadened the political space for long-term stability and democracy.

On a comparative basis, Ethiopia has been very successful in conducting low-cost elections. The considerable international electoral assistance the country has received over the years is a significant variable in keeping the cost of elections low. But, perhaps, the most critical explanation for this state of affairs is the fact that the National Electoral Board makes use of the huge state bureaucracy and the civil services at central, regional and lower levels of government to administer elections. While this might have kept the costs down, it has serious implications for the legitimacy of election outcomes and the extent to which such support from the state and government will favor ruling party candidates.

6. Conclusions

In view of the preceding discussion, the following conclusions are provided.

Despite political party assistance and the original installation of a broad-based coalition, Ethiopia has remained a one-party dominated state. As noted earlier, the regime has not been able to broaden its political space to include opposition parties that can offer alternatives to the electorate.

Although some positive changes have taken place in state-society relations in Ethiopia, such as the burgeoning private print media and growth of civil society organizations, the political regime that emerged over the past 12 years has failed to broaden its political space and create a level playing field for free and competitive elections for all contestants. Albeit the international gesture to institutionalize democratic politics, therefore, state and society in post-Mengistu Ethiopia are under the tight grip of one-party rule.

In Ethiopia, national, regional and local/woreda elections have been conducted with the assistance of a government-managed electoral authority. This can insure the election of ruling party candidates and has serious implications for the legitimacy of outcomes as the true expression of the wish of the people.

Ethiopia uses an electoral practice that operates on the basis a plurality of votes cast in single member constituencies. This practice precludes the representation of candidates having alternative programs and minority and disadvantaged parties other than the winning candidate with the highest number of votes. In electoral systems that do not provide for a level playing field, such as Ethiopia's current system, this practice can give undue advantage to the party in power especially when the government has complete control over the mass media and other state resources and uses the same to influence the outcome of the elections in its favor.

In several discussions with the authors, most opposition parties in Ethiopia have severely criticized the current single member constituency system as being undemocratic and favoring the ruling party. They have repeatedly called for changes to the constitution to allow for 'proportional representation, which makes it possible to share parliamentary seats among different political forces in proportion to their electoral strength. In principle, no political force or part of public opinion retains a monopoly; at the same time, none is excluded from representation. Hence, the system's main virtue is said to be justice. Another advantage of this system is that voting takes place in a single round and the 'politicking and bickering', which often takes place in systems practicing a second round, is avoided (IPU 1993).

Ethiopia's National Electoral Board has been given formal statutory independence. However, this was no guarantee for its effective functioning as a neutral body free from outside influence, especially the executive.

Insufficient voter education, voter apathy and the absence of a united and strong opposition are constraining factors in democratizing the election process in Ethiopia.

Despite the consistently high voter turnout in many of the elections in Ethiopia, civic education remains weak and insufficient, especially in the rural areas.

Ethiopia's National Electoral Board has been given formal statutory independence. However, this was no guarantee for its effective functioning as a neutral body free from outside influence, especially the executive.

III. INTERNATIONAL HUMAN RIGHTS ASSISTANCE

1. Background: History of Human Rights Violations

As noted above, neither the Imperial nor the Derg regime allowed opposition parties, an independent press, nor civil society organizations except some professional associations and NGOs; these latter were restricted to emergency relief and the provision of health and other social services to communities in need. While, in both regimes, the formal constitutions provided a wide variety of civil liberties (including the rights to freedom of expression and of assembly), in practice none of these liberties were enjoyed by citizens. Both were highly authoritarian regimes and dissent or the public expression of independent opinion was not tolerated. Students were the only group who from the mid-1960s onwards gave voice to public discontent as well as to the need for reforms and social justice. Student demonstrations, which became frequent occurrences towards the end of the decade and in the first year of the Derg, were violently suppressed and many student leaders were placed in detention without the decision of the courts.

There were extensive human rights violations during the Imperial regime but their nature was somewhat different from that of the two subsequent regimes. While there were cases of illegal detentions, disappearances and torture, the most widespread form of injustice had to do with the illegal expropriation of the property (especially landed property) of groups, communities and individuals[13]. There were large-scale dispossession of peasants and their eviction from the land, in particular in areas settled by minority nationalities. This was frequently the work of powerful landed interests as well as members of the royal family. The Imperial state expropriated large tracts of rangeland, forests and other resources from pastoralists and other communities on the dubious ground that these resources had no recognized owner(s) with legal title to them. In this country as well as elsewhere in Africa, communities and individuals have had claims to land and other natural resources based on long established and legitimate customary rights but such rights were frequently disregarded in Ethiopia when it suited the government or powerful elements of the ruling class. There were also many cases of unjust treatment of persons suspected of plotting against the government, and

---

[13] For this and the discussion of the Derg period below, see references in Chapter 1

the expropriation of the property of dissidents or opposition groups was quite common.

The evidence regarding human rights violations during the Derg is relatively better. While the military dictatorship did not welcome international human rights organizations to investigate the human rights situation in the country, a few of them, including Amnesty International, managed to get access to information on the basis of which they issued very critical reports detailing extensive human rights violations. Large-scale extra-judicial killings, mass arrests, and disappearances were reported, together with the suppression of rights of free expression and assembly. The plight of prominent members of the royal family, and of Ethiopian academics and dissidents who were imprisoned without due process and the right to appear before a court, were frequently highlighted. The so-called Red Terror, which the Derg unleashed in the latter part of the 1970s in an attempt to crush its opponents, was universally condemned by the international human rights movement as well as by many Western governments. The Derg's massive resettlement program which was under way from the early 1980s, drew strong criticism from a number of human rights groups, some of whom compared it to the forced labor camp system of the Stalin era (see Dessalegn 2003b).

There is broad consensus among Ethiopian social scientists and historians that the Derg was one of the most oppressive and despotic regimes in the country's history. The regime came to power through peaceful means but was to stay in power by the indiscriminate and unrestrained use of violence and terror. The victims of repression were not, by and large, a particular group, community or class, but a cross-section of society, both rural and urban, civilian as well as military and security forces. In the end, it was its unrestrained violence and terror that was to alienate the majority of the population, undermine its authority and finally lead to its ignominious collapse. A catalogue of its brutality against the citizenry of this country during the seventeen years of its rule would be too long to list here but we provide below some of the most shocking cases of human rights violations perpetrated under the regime[14].

- Summary executions of over one hundred high ranking government and military officials immediately after the Derg's seizure of power; subsequent executions of several dozen

---

[14] The list is based on personal experience of the authors; press reports during the Derg; and references cited in Chapter 1 above.

members of the ruling class alleged to have fomented rebellions.

- Violent suppression of trade union, student, and other peaceful demonstrations in the mid-1970s in which many people were injured or killed, and large numbers arrested. In the demonstrations organized by one of the opposition groups in 1976, several hundred young people are reported to have been massacred by security forces.

- Intimidation, detention and torture of hundreds of civil servants and public enterprise management officials "suspected" of bureaucratic red-tape, economic sabotage, or alleged to have carried out counter-revolutionary activities.

- Arbitrary arrest and imprisonment without trial of men, women and children from all walks of life numbering in the hundreds of thousands before and during the Red Terror in the second half of the 1970s.

- Executions of people suspected of belonging to the opposition during the so-called Red Terror numbering in the thousands.

- Intimidation and harassment of followers of several Protestants denominations and the closure of many of their churches and religious institutions.

- Over 30,000 deaths of peasants involved in the government's forced resettlement scheme in the years between 1984 and 1986; deaths due to hunger, disease and exhaustion during the relocation process and immediately after (Dessalegn 2003b).

- Forced recruitment of hundreds of thousands of young men, in particular peasants, to fight in the various fronts opened up by ethnic-based rebel insurgency in the 1970s. The ill-fated Peasant Militia offensive launched by the Derg in 1975 against the Eritrean rebels resulted in disaster, and casualties among the militia, many of whom were forcibly recruited, were enormous.

It is worth noting here that the atrocities committed by the Derg are in some ways comparable to those committed by Pol Pot in Cambodia.

2. Post Conflict Human Rights Context

When the Derg was finally overthrown, there was public expectations that the country would make a fresh start and the atrocities and mass terror of the past would not be repeated. While there was considerable apprehension regarding the ethnic policies of the new regime, there

51

was hope that human rights violations on the order of the past would not be repeated. The Constitution of the new regime, which came into force in 1995, guaranteed a wide range of human rights and freedoms, including the right to freedom of expression, of assembly and respect for the rule of law. However, what was guaranteed in the constitution and the measures the government has taken since to deal with its opponents, real or imagined, and the political decisions undertaken were highly contradictory. As we shall see below, there were numerous cases of unlawful killings and arbitrary detentions, the rule of law was frequently ignored, political organizations not based on ethnic identity (such as pan-Ethiopian parties) were not allowed, and the registration and activities of civil society organizations were restricted. Some of these constitutional restrictions have been eased during the second half of the new government, partly as a result of the Ethio-Eritrean war, and partly due to the conflict within the ruling party, and the purge of party and state officials that followed.

The human rights record of the present government, measured by most accepted standards, has been very poor, though, as we noted above, comparison between it and the two other regimes that preceded it is difficult to make. It can be said, however, that mass atrocities on the scale perpetrated by the Derg have not been committed so far. Another important difference is that at present an independent press has been allowed, and civil society institutions, including rights-based advocacy organizations, which would have been unthinkable at the time of the Imperial or Derg regimes, are becoming part of the socio-political landscape. A third difference to be noted is that while not exactly invited to the country by the authorities, international human rights organizations have been able to send monitors to gather information and to report on the human rights situation in the country.

International human rights organizations such as Amnesty International (AI), Human Rights Watch, Africa Watch (AW), and others have issued numerous reports on the government's record and the state of human rights in the country. Amnesty in particular has issued frequent reports since the mid-1990s highlighting numerous cases of illegal detentions, torture, threats to press freedom and the arrest of journalists, mass deportations of citizens of Eritrean origin (54,000 according to one of its reports), and disappearances (AI website). Similarly, Human Rights Watch, Africa Watch and the U.S. Department of State have produced reports on the country at least once a year. In the latest report available, the first two organizations argue that human right conditions have not markedly improved in 2002, and go on to document a wide diversity of cases of violations;

on the other hand, the report prepared by the State Department points out that the rights record remains poor but there have been improvements in a few areas.

One should note here that despite the fact that international organizations are able to gather information more or less freely at present, their reports are deficient in some respects and contain many inaccuracies. Such organizations are understandably constrained by a number of factors chief of which is the lack of a deeper understanding of the political process in the country, the inability to follow events closely and to ensure the accuracy of information received and the credibility of informants. None of these organizations have local representation here although EHRCO is affiliated with a number of them; on many occasions the former depend on the reports published by the latter.

EHRCO has been monitoring the human rights situation in the country and issuing reports on rights violations since it was first established in 1991. The main violations frequently reported on include cases of extra-judicial killings, illegal detentions, disappearances, torture, unlawful expropriation of property, threats to freedom of the press and harassment and detention of journalists. The following table is based on a tally of reported violations that occurred from 1991 to 2000 that appear in EHRCO's two published volumes (1999; 2003).

Table 3.1 **Human Rights Violations 1991-2000**

Type of Violations	No. in Period 1991-97	No. in Period 1997-2000
Extra-judicial Killings	185	141
Torture	70	31
Disappearances	120	30
Illegal Detentions	5525	1052

Source: EHRCO 1999, 2003

The Table does not include what EHRCO describes as massacres that occurred on a number of occasions in different parts of the country, of which the main ones have been in the towns of Areka, Gonder, Tepi, Awassa, and in Addis Ababa following the peaceful demonstration of students. In all these cases, no measures were taken on the security forces responsible for the human rights violations.

Let us look briefly at some of the most serious cases of violations discussed at length by EHRCO (1999, 2003). It is of course impossible to include all the violations reported by the organization given the limitations of space. The massacre in Areka (a small town in south central Ethiopia) occurred on 14 July 1992 when security forces opened fire on a peaceful demonstration by demobilized soldiers demanding stipends which they had been promised but which they had not received. EHRCO quotes a report by a Parliamentary fact finding mission as saying that 31 persons were killed and 29 wounded but it suspects the casualty figures are higher. The 1993 massacre in Gonder, a large town in northwest Ethiopia, also led to a large number of innocent civilians being hurt. The incident occurred when security forces shot into a peaceful assembly of worshippers at a church in the process of trying to arrest a priest of the church. EHRCO puts the casualty figures at 18 civilians killed and 17 wounded. The conflict in Tepi in southwestern Ethiopia occurred in March 2002 when two ethnic groups clashed due to political rivalry. In the ensuing clash, security forces, including soldiers and a special police force brought into the area by the authorities, opened fire indiscriminately, leading to many deaths and thousands of people displaced from their homes. EHRCO lists the names of 24 people, including 4 security officers, as having been killed in the clash; some 4738 people are believed to have been displaced. The violence in Awassa, a town in south central Ethiopia, in which security forces opened fire on a peaceful crowd demonstrating against the decision of the local authority to relocate the seat of the Regional government elsewhere, led to the death and injury of scores of civilians and the arrest of over thirty-five demonstrators.

Addis Ababa has witnessed a considerable number of clashes between the authorities and different sections of the population, but for our purposes it is enough to cite two examples. The first incident was the violent suppression of the protest of businessmen in the city. The capital's business community was quite upset when in 1996 the government decided to raise rents of offices, shops, stalls and other business premises by a substantial margin. The government owns a majority of the city's buildings, offices and rental houses and most people are tenants of the state. The business community decided to hold a peaceful demonstration to express its grievances on 17 May 1997. This was followed by a strike, which closed down most shops, trading centers and business offices a few days later. The government reacted angrily and used strong-arm methods to quash the protests. According to EHRCO, 84 alleged leaders were placed in detention and the licenses of 52 of them were revoked as a retaliatory measure (EHRCO 1999: 276ff). Many of the detained were not released until many weeks later.

The second example concerns the violent suppression of students in Addis Ababa, in particular Addis Ababa University students in 1993, again in 1997 and in 2001. In all cases, the government used violent methods to stop students and other young people to stage peaceful demonstrations. In these incidents dozens of students were hurt and several hundred arrested. EHRCO reports, for example, that in the last incident, 10 people including students were killed, and over 200 students arrested.

The government's response to EHRCO's report has changed over the years. Initially, it was one of hostility accompanied by attempts to silence the organizations (see below). The government accused EHRCO of prejudice against the new political order and being a political organization rather than an impartial human rights group. Later, it sought to belittle the reports by ignoring them and refusing to respond to the allegations. This soft approach was in part to due the change of leadership at EHRCO in the last quarter of the 1990s and the war with Eritrea. Table 3.1 above shows that the number of human rights violations has decreased in the second period shown. We hesitate to conclude from this that this is evidence of improvements in the human rights record of the government, although it may be suggested that while the overall record is still very poor the second period is not as bad as the first.

3. International Assistance to Human Rights

a. Human Rights Observation

Among many donors in this country, human rights falls within their democracy or good governance assistance program and thus it is not always easy to disentangle how much support has been provided for human rights causes per se. Human rights does not have defined boundaries in many cases and is seen as a cross-cutting issue. For instance, there is a donor Human Rights Subgroup in the country, consisting of members from a large number of countries. The Subgroup meets regularly to discuss 'human rights' issues in the country. The Subgroup is further divided into four sub-committees concerned with elections, the press, freedom of association and labor, and freedom of belief and conscience. Thus, the remit of the Subgroup is quite broad.

There is another donor body that also monitors human rights in the country. This is made up of EU member states and the European Commission Delegation in the country. This group also meets regularly at ambassadorial level or lower, depending on the gravity of the matter to be discussed. The Embassy of the country which holds the EU presidency acts as the 'leader' of the group and convenes meetings, sets the agenda, and often influences the debate. A presidency country with a strong concern for human rights may influence the EU to be more engaged with human rights. On the other hand, a presidency with different concerns may have a different effect on the members. The EU group has more clout than the Human Rights Subgroup noted above, however, it takes a long time to arrive at a decision acceptable to all as each member state has to agree to the terms of the decision.

It should be noted that the EC's engagement with issues of human rights and democratization was given the green light only after the Cotonou Agreement with the ACP countries in 2000. Previous to that, the EC was restricted in its mandate since its relationship was only with the government and the areas of its engagement excluded human rights and 'political' issues. Thus the EC was not able to make a strategic intervention in the democratization process taking place in the country and was limited to providing low level support to a few minor initiatives. Article 8 of the Cotonou Agreement now specifies that the EC and the governments concerned should engage in political dialogue which encompasses regular assessments concerning respect for human rights, democratic principles, the rule of law and good governance. Moreover, the EC has also been mandated to work with non-state actors under Article 4 of the Agreement (EC 2000). Such actors include civil society organizations, the private sector, and others. This will obviously have an impact on resource allocation.

The donor community employs several methods of monitoring the human rights situation in the country. When serious violations occur, as it did in 2002 in Awassa in the south of the country, and in Tepi in the southwest (see above), the donor's Human Rights Subgroup as well as the EC send a fact finding mission to gather information and to discuss the matter with all the parties to the incidents involved. The Subgroup does not make a decision or take any measures, it only provides information to the members; it is the responsibility of each donor or country to make its own decisions[15]. The EC on the other hand can take measures under certain circumstances. Another way donors monitor the human rights situation is through the work of the international human rights

---

[15] Interview with L. Williams of the British Embassy, and O. Blake of DFID, Addis Ababa. Ms. Williams argued that the fact that the Subgroup does not make decisions should not be seen as a weakness.

movement, in particular Amnesty, Human Rights Watch, and others. Finally, the donor community also relies on the work of local human rights groups, in particular the reports prepared by EHRCO.

b. Red Terror Tribunals

The EPRDF government arrested and brought charges against nearly 8,000 officials of the Derg regime for genocide, war crimes, and atrocities soon after it came to power. The officials included high government and security personnel as well as lowly state functionaries; a few, including Mengistu Haile Mariam, were tried in absentia. The court cases related to 'genocide' during the Red Terror of the mid-1970s, and war crimes allegedly committed in Tigrai in 1987 during the Derg's military offensive against the TPLF. These cases are still in progress in the federal and Regional courts, though some of the accused have been freed or sentenced. Assistance to the InterAfrica Group, a Regional NGO with its head office in Addis Ababa, was provided by Amnesty and other international human rights organizations to record the proceedings and provide transcripts and other pertinent information about the cases to the wider public (interview with Jalal A Latif).

The trials have not been received favorably by the public for a number of reasons: a) because they were seen to be politically motivated; it was seen as a trial imposed by the victor on a defeated opponent; b) because the prosecution was carried out by the government's Special Prosecutor's Office, and the judges were government appointed judges and not independent ones; neither during the Derg regime nor at present has the judiciary been an independent institution; and c) because there were strong suspicions, which the government did very little to allay, that the outcome was already determined and most of the accused would be convicted anyway (local press reports).

4. Legal and Institutional Reforms

a. Structure of the Court System

An independent and effective judiciary is an essential element in promoting democracy, good governance and the rule of law in Ethiopia. It is necessary to review the Ethiopian justice system for effective donor intervention to build the capacity of the justice sector as part of the broad assistance program to democracy and human rights.

The judiciary in Ethiopia has a three-tier system of courts. These are the Federal Supreme Court, Federal High Court and Federal First Instant Court. The organization of courts at Regional levels is the same as that of the federal court system. In 2002, there were a total of 111 judges serving at the three tiers of the federal court system. There were 14, 32 and 65 judges serving at Federal Supreme, Federal High and Federal First Instant courts respectively. Out of this total, 35 or about 32 percent were women.

b. Recruitment and Independence of the Judicial System

The mode of recruitment and appointment of judges is a critical factor in determining the effectiveness of the judiciary in upholding the rule of law and human rights. In addition, it can also determine the integrity and independence of the system in dispensing justice. One means of guaranteeing the independence of the judiciary is through the appointment and promotion of judges. In Ethiopia, the Constitution formally provides for an independent judiciary that is free from external influence in the administration of justice. As a guarantee to provide for the independence and integrity of the judiciary, the responsibility for the recruitment and promotion of judges in Ethiopia is shared between the parliament and the executive.

At the federal level, judges are appointed by the House of Peoples' Representatives upon submission of a list of nominees by the Prime Minister initially screened by the Federal Judicial Administration Commission. The same procedure is followed at the Regional level whereby the screening and selection is performed by the Regional Judicial Administration Commissions and the final appointment granted by the Regional Assemblies. The criteria for being appointed as a federal judge are rigorous and a candidate must satisfy the following: attain the age of 25; have legal training; be loyal to the constitution; consent to be a judge; have good reputation for diligence; have a sense of justice; and have good conduct.

As noted earlier, the State Council of the Region appoints the president and vice-presidents of the State Supreme Court upon the recommendation by the Chief Executive of the Regional State (Art. 81(3) Federal Constitution). It is also provided that the State Council shall appoint the other judges upon the recommendation by the Regional State Judicial Administration Council. However, it is incumbent upon the State Judicial Administration Council to solicit and obtain the views of the Federal Judicial Administration Council on the nominees and forward these views along with its recommendations before submitting nominations to the State Council.

As a measure to guarantee the independence and integrity of the judiciary, the Ethiopian Constitution has provided for lifetime appointment of judges. For Example, article 79 of the Federal Constitution provides that no judge shall be removed from his/her duties before s/he reaches the retirement age determined by law except under some specified circumstances. Accordingly, the tenure of any judge can be terminated only: a) upon resignation subject to a two-month prior notice; b) upon reaching the retirement age of 60 years; c) where it is decided that he/she is incapable of properly discharging his/her duties due to illness; d) he/she has committed a breach of discipline; e) it is decided that he/she has a manifest incompetence and inefficiency; and, f) he/she has transgressed the Disciplinary and Code of Conduct Rules of judges.

In 2000, the Ethiopian government launched a justice system reform program to improve the system and process of judicial administration. The reform is guided by the conviction that a predictable legal environment with an objective, reliable and independent judiciary is an essential factor for democratization, good governance and human rights. A related objective of the reform program is the establishment of a secure basis for the rule of law so that basic democratic and human rights are respected (Ministry of Justice, 2002).

The reform program plans to remove impediments of access to justice at all levels. This will be achieved by making legal services less expensive, justice institutions more accessible, ensuring that legal services are not time consuming, formalistic and full of procedural pitfalls, and that execution is not delayed. It is also important that the justice system has to be responsive to the needs of the people (Ministry of Justice, 2002).

The government's judicial reform program is an important measure to promote democracy and the rule of law and has received considerable bilateral and multilateral assistance. The project has three components: training, court administration reform and law reform and revision. The objectives and achievements of the program so far and the amount of external assistance provided for the project are discussed as follows.

c. Training

There is at present an acute shortage of adequately trained and qualified judges in Ethiopia and this has severely affected the justice sector. Providing assistance to the legal sector should be an area of high priority in so far as this falls within the framework of assistance to human rights, good governance and democracy. A well-functioning legal system that can protect human rights and uphold the rule of law is also a goal expressed by the Constitution of the Federal Democratic Republic of Ethiopia (FDRE).

The problems of the justice sector were exacerbated and its capacity crippled following the mass dismissal of judges by the Prime Minister in the early 1990s on corruption allegations. Over the years, the shortage of trained and well-qualified judges has resulted in court delays and massive backlog cases which cannot be redressed in the not-to-distant future. More important, the delays and inefficiencies in the court system have had serious implications for the rule of law in the country and the right of the citizenry to be given quick justice.

To remedy the situation, the Government of Ethiopia in cooperation with foreign donors had initiated a judicial training program in early 2000. For example, there is the program launched by the Federal Supreme Court in collaboration with Regional Supreme Courts and USAID aimed at: providing training programs to judges to improve their capacity in all fields; strengthening the institutional capacity by providing materials that are needed by judges in their day-to-day activities; and making all the preparations for the establishment of a permanent Judicial Training Unit (JTU). Major funding for the program came from the USAID to the tune of 500,000 US Dollars and was conducted by Ethiopian and expatriate legal professionals. The full cost of the program and the number of participants are provided in Table 3.3.

Table 3.3 **No. of Participants in Judicial Training Program**
2000-2003

No.	Name of Court	No. of Trainees	Amount in US D
1.	Federal Supreme & High Courts, Addis Ababa Municipal Courts	150	7,944.44
2.	Afar Region Supreme Court & High Courts	64	68,921.52
3.	Amhara Region Supreme & High Courts	132	91,535.89
4.	Benishangul-Gumuz Supreme Court & High Courts	50	35,990.64
5.	Oromiya Region Supreme & High Courts	107	70,827.64
6.	Tigray Region Supreme & High Courts	50	39,981.88
7.	Gambella Region Supreme & High Courts	33	22,793.63
8.	SNNPR Supreme & High Courts	150	98,656.42
9.	Harari Region Supreme & High Courts	15	11,521.48
10.	Somali Region Supreme & High courts	50	34,298.00
	Total	801	482,470.66

Source: Federal Supreme Court 2003

A total of 801 judges from the Federal and Regional Supreme and High Courts benefited from the training. USAID was the major provider of the assistance and actively cooperated with the Federal Supreme Court's Judicial Training Unit in successfully conducting the training project. It was indeed a major piece of achievement in enhancing the capacity of the judiciary in upholding human rights and the rule of law. Equally important, the program could be assessed as highly successful and effectively coordinated and institutionalized between the Ministry of Justice and the USAID.

d. Court Administration Reform

Side by side with the training of judges, the government also undertook a Court Administration Reform project with the assistance of CIDA Canada. The total cost of the project was said to be

157,000 US dollars. The goal of the project is to "contribute to the stability, security and sustained development of Ethiopia by promoting practices that will help achieve and sustain the rule of law". More specifically, the project aims to reduce administrative inefficiencies and develop Ethiopian courts, promote better management practices, and promote greater equity and judicial independence. In sum, the project was aimed at exploring ways and means of improving the efficiency and effectiveness of the operation and management of the courts. Pilot projects for the improvement of the court system at the federal level have been implemented. The benefits of the pilot projects at the Supreme Court will be gradually replicated at the lower federal and Regional courts, and this will go a long way in reforming the justice system.

e. Law Reform and Revision

The Government has established the Justice and Legal System Research Institute under the Ministry of Justice to undertake a comprehensive law reform and revision program to harmonize existing laws with the constitution and thereby enhance democracy and socio-economic development (Mandefrot, 2002). A major component of this program i is developing improved court management and administration systems throughout the Federal Supreme Court, other federal courts, and selected regional and local courts. The Canadian International Development Agency (CIDA) has been a major funder of this project to the tune of 3,850,000 US dollars. CIDA has commissioned the Canadian Office of the Commissioner for Federal Judicial Affairs as the implementing agency, whose support will help to reduce administrative inefficiencies and delays. Upon the successful completion of this project, it is expected that new and improved court administration systems will contribute to more efficient disposition of cases and improved court professional and operational standards. This will further support better-performing courts, and a strengthened rule of law in Ethiopia.

In addition to the above, a number of foreign governments have provided assistance to enhance the capacity of the Ethiopian justice sector. For example, the French Government has provided experts to assist the Ethiopian Ministry of Capacity Building in training prosecutors and facilitating legislative reform. The total cost of the program was estimated at 500,000 US dollars and would run until 2004. The Norwegian Government was actively involved in enhancing the capacity of the Federal Prosecutor's Office. They were also supporting a program of training in human rights, good governance and the rule of law.[16]

f. Parliament's Capacity Building

As part of the democracy and governance project, the Canadian Government has provided considerable assistance to the tune of 3,850,000 US dollars to enhance the governance and accountability of the Federal Parliament of Ethiopia. Funded under the Donor Group Cooperation Framework, the Canadian Parliamentary Centre was selected as the implementing agency covering the period 1999-2004. The project targets four key areas: strengthening of the Parliamentary Committee Processes, particularly the finance, legal and women's affairs committees; master planning, public consultation, and establishment of the Human Rights Commission and Office of Ombudsman; assistance in the creation of a parliamentary centre for research and public consultation; and democratic outreach, to support an enhanced process for dialogue and engagement of Parliament and civil society in the democratization in Ethiopia. An assessment of the project made in September, 2001, indicated positive outcomes: parliamentary leaders have become more committed to institutional development; members are more aware of what MPs should be doing; committees are emerging as significant work units; the physical infrastructure has been upgraded; and there is increasing awareness among groups in civil society and donors about the importance of parliament as an important venue for the discussion of national issues (Nakamura, 2001).

5. Impact of International Assistance on the Justice Sector and Parliament

There has been significant bilateral assistance to the justice sector in Ethiopia in the areas of training of judges and improving the overall efficiency of the system for the administration of justice. For a

---

[16] Interview with Ato Mandefrot Belay

number of reasons, however, the assistance has had little impact in terms of promoting the rule of law or enhancing the independence of the judiciary in dispensing justice. Despite formal constitutional guarantees for its independence and integrity, the judiciary in Ethiopia is in practice subservient to a domineering executive. Hence, capacity building in the form of training judges and improving the administrative infrastructure must be accompanied by fundamental institutional reform that provides for an effective checks and balances system between the executive and the judiciary to yield the intended result of judicial independence.

At present, judges in Ethiopia are nominated by the executive branch of government and their appointment is made by a legislature made up of members of the ruling party. This practice has affected the integrity and independence of the court system from the influence of the executive and the legislature. Hence, major reform initiatives to streamline the appointment and recruitment of judges and make the process free from the influence of the dominant executive is a desirable alternative. Second, assistance for judicial reform must be delivered as one essential component of a total assistance package that includes: projects to improve the overall human rights situation in the country, such as human rights education to law officers/police; programs to expand legal education at the national level; and the establishment and strengthening of Ombudsman/woman offices and independent human rights monitoring organizations in the country.

International assistance to capacity building of the National Parliament has enhanced the administrative and institutional structure of the legislature but has not transformed it into an effective institution to hold the executive accountable nor to make this organ of government an active partner in public policy making. Formally, the Ethiopian parliament is independent of external influence in its legislative responsibility. It has the power of legislation on all matters assigned by the Federal Constitution (Art. 55(1). In practice, however, parliament is a dormant institution and its role as the forum for debating issues of national importance independent of the influence of the executive is very limited. It has largely functioned as an appendage of the Executive thanks to the fact that the overwhelming majority of the members of parliament are members of the EPRDF ruling party, which controls both the legislative and executive branches of government.

6. Impact of Electoral Assistance on Civil Society Organizations

As explained elsewhere in this report, civil society organizations that uphold the rule of law and play an advocacy role are new to the Ethiopian political landscape. Traditionally, the country has limited experience in involving non-state actors in the policy process but over the past 10-12 years the country has seen a burgeoning of independent civil society organizations. Successive governments in the past have pursued a state-centered political agenda and non-state actors were viewed with suspicion at best and down right hostility at worst. Hence, their role in promoting democracy and respect for human rights has indeed been limited. It is still incumbent upon the political system to open up and demonstrate a clear commitment to entertain alternative voices in public policy that come from independent civil society.

Ethiopia has comparatively fewer civil society institutions than many African countries. Further, many of these institutions have not developed their own programs to act independently, and experience capacity and resource constraints to play a constructive role to advance democracy. Despite the hurdles, however, there are some civil society organizations, such as the Ethiopian Human Rights Council (EHRCO), the Ethiopian Women Lawyers Association (EWLA), the Ethiopian Economic Policy Research Institute (EEPRI), the Forum for Social Studies (FSS), Christian Relief and Development Association (CRDA), to name only a few, which have emerged as non-partisan civil society institutions and act as independent voices of the public and have thus exerted some indirect impact in advancing democracy, human rights and the rule of law in the country (Dessalegn, 2002; Inter-Africa Group, 2000).

In Ethiopia, civil society institutions can operate only if they are duly registered with the Ministry of Justice. There are detailed legal provisions and procedures for the registration of civil society organizations as provided in Article 479 of the Civil Code of 1960. The law stipulates that:

> no association shall carry on any activities other than those necessary to effect the establishment there of unless and until the memorandum of association or statutes therefore of have been registered in accordance with the law and these regulations and a Certificate of Registration has been issued to the founders thereof pursuant to Article 9 hereof. Any person

acting on behalf of or in the name of an association not so registered shall be jointly and severally liable with the association for any such acts.

Despite the hurdles and lack of a conducive political environment, there are some civil society organizations which have been quite active in advocating for human rights, the rule of law, and monitoring elections. Two of these are the Ethiopian Human Rights Council (EHRCO) and the Christian Relief and Development Association (CRDA) -an umbrella organization for NGOs mainly engaged in relief and development. Both of these organizations have received substantial external assistance and have been quite active in election monitoring and voter education programs during the 2000 national elections.

The Ethiopian Human Rights Council (EHRCO)

The Ethiopian Human Rights Council (EHRCO) is an independent, non-governmental, non-profit making, non-partisan and non-political organization established in 1991. The founding members are Ethiopians from all walks of life -- academics, professionals and businessmen--who are committed to the cause of human rights, rule of law and democracy. EHRCO's membership spreads to other parts of Africa, Europe, the United States of America and Canada, and these are several EHRCO support committees in major cities of Europe, the U.S.A. and Canada. In addition, EHRCO exchanges reports and information with international and continental human rights organizations, such as Amnesty International (AI), Africa Watch (AW), World Organization Against Torture (WOAT) and the International Federation of Human Rights (IFHR) (for more details of the organization's history, see below).

EHRCO has three fundamental and inseparable objectives:
- To strive for the establishment of the democratic process;
- To promote the rule of law and due process;
- To encourage the respect for and to monitor violations of human rights in Ethiopia.

EHRCO also has other objectives, including the following:
- encouraging Ethiopia's acceptance of all international conventions, covenants, charters and declarations that are

66

concerned with human rights;

- organizing seminars, workshops, panel discussions and lectures in order to promote the respect for human rights, the rule of law and the democratic process; and,
- publishing and disseminating periodicals, newsletters and books in order to elucidate and advance the cause of human rights and the democratic process.

The basic mission of EHRCO is to monitor human rights violations in the country. It receives considerable international financial support from the Governments of the Norway, Sweden, Finland, the Netherlands, Switzerland and United Kingdom. EHRCO was one of the few civil society organizations that was active in monitoring the 2000 elections. International assistance for its work came from the Embassies of Finland, Norway, the Netherlands and Sweden based in Addis Ababa. It organized public lectures and panel discussions on different topics throughout the country prior to the elections. It also launched civic and voter education programs that focused on democracy and elections, measures and standards for fair and free elections, campaign issues, role of the media in democratic elections. The reports issued by the organization indicated that a sizable segment of the public attended these panel discussions and seminars.

The main area of involvement of EHRCO in the 2000 elections was in monitoring and observing the election process. In the end, it was sharply critical of the May 2000 elections and has characterized the same as 'neither free nor fair'. The organization registered 182 election violations during the registration period; and most of these incidents involved arbitrary killings, illegal detentions, illegal dismissals/transfer from jobs of opposition and independent candidates and harassment of candidates. In its damning assessment, the organization reported that 'the large majority of election officials, support staff, security personnel, and even the so called people's observers were not neutral and objective because often they favored ruling party/government candidates' (EHRCO, 2002).

There were other civic society organizations that were active in voter education programs in the 2000 national elections with support received from the international community. Two examples included the Christian Relief Development Association (CRDA) and the Addis Ababa and Ethiopian Chambers of Commerce. It is not necessary to provide a detailed account of the activities of these and other civil society organizations because they are not human rights

67

organizations and most of their work focused on civic education rather than election monitoring and supervision. In addition, donor assistance for voter and civic education programs prior to the 2000 national elections has been discussed in the section dealing with international electoral assistance.

7. Human Rights Institutions

a. Overview

One can identify several sectors or institutions which have a human rights mandate and which have benefited from donor assistance. Donor assistance to human rights has primarily been financial assistance to advocacy organizations on the one hand, and financial support as well as training and technical support to government institutions on the other. Assistance has been provided for: a) preparatory work for the setting up a government human right commission and ombudsman institution; b) reform of legal institutions, and training of law enforcement agencies; c) support to legislative bodies and training of legislators; d) financial support to civil society organizations active in monitoring human rights, human rights protection and advocacy.

b. Human Rights Commission/Ombudsman

It was towards the end of the 1990s that the government made some positive gestures regarding the setting up of a human rights commission and the office of an ombudsman. Both institutions are eagerly awaited by civil society organizations as well as by donors, who are keen to finance them in the belief that they would go some way to improve the human rights situation in the country. However, the government has shown a marked reluctance to move the process along and to facilitate the setting up of the offices concerned. The legislation creating the Ethiopian Human Rights Commission and also the Institution of the Ombudsman went through Parliament in the first half of 2000, but the physical establishment of the institutions has been delayed since then, and at present there is no indication when they will start to carry out their duties.

The legislations are sound as they stand: both the Commission and the Office of the Ombudsman have been created as autonomous organizations accountable to Parliament. In both, the chief officers are nominated by nominating committees and appointed by the Lower

House with a term of office of five years (FDRE 2000). This is meant to give the officials concerned some degree of freedom of action and some protection from pressure from the Executive branch. The government's lack of enthusiasm to see these institutions come into being has to do with the fact that it does not have any leverage over them and that it is not quite confident of its human rights record.

On the other hand, the government was quick to set up the Federal Ethics and Anti-Corruption Commission. Newspaper columnists and others have alleged that the speedy establishment of the Commission had an ulterior motive: it was meant to be used as an instrument against the opposition within the ruling party following the internal power conflict in which many party stalwarts were subsequently purged from the organization. Some of the purged officials were later arrested under charges of corruption brought by the newly established Commission; some are still in detention today and their court case is making painfully slow progress. The legislation, which was adopted in 2001, gives wide powers to the Commission to investigate alleged cases of corruption, to detain suspects without a court order, to summon persons in public office, public and private enterprises and receive testimony from them. The Commission is accountable to the Prime Minister and the chief officials are appointed by Parliament upon his nomination (FDRE 2001). Since its establishment, the Commission has been actively engaged in investigating numerous public agencies, and has brought charges of malpractice and corruption against over 150 persons some of whom have been detained and all whom are awaiting trial as of the end of 2002 (FEAC 2003). So far, donors have not been keen to support the Commission and budget allocation from the government has been the organization's sole source of funds for its activities.

c. Human Rights Organizations

We may first begin by a brief note on the broader context within which to view human rights organizations that have emerged in this country. The voluntary sector in Ethiopia has been growing at a rapid pace in the last six to seven years. There is today a wide diversity of non-government institutions, many of which would not have been allowed to function either under the Imperial or Derg regimes. The voluntary sector now consists of professional societies, women's groups, human rights and advocacy organizations, community organizations, indigenous and Northern NGOs, employers' associations, educational foundations, think tanks, and cultural societies.

Human rights organizations in Ethiopia are those whose activities focus primarily on what may be described broadly as "rights" issues: promoting respect for the rule of law, and protecting the rights of citizens specially women; enhancing civic awareness through civic education and human rights training. For the purposes of this study we may divide the human rights organizations in the country into four broad categories based on their main sphere of activity and mandate. These consist of:

- those that monitor human rights violations and prepare public reports on them (for example EHRCO);
- those that defend the rights of women (eg. EWLA);
- those that generally enhance public awareness about civil liberties and promote respect for the rule of law by providing human rights training to officials in law enforcement agencies, etc.; (eg. APAP)
- those that undertake civic education, in particular voter education to enable citizens to make the right decisions during elections (eg. CLCBS).

We shall look closely at both EHRCO and EWLA since they are the most prominent human rights organizations in the country. But a word about APAP because it is an important rights-based organization and because it shares one important factor in common with the others. All three organizations were at one time or another harassed by the authorities, and closed down or threatened with closure because of the kind of work they were doing. In all cases, few donors raised their voice to remonstrate or show concern except perhaps a small number of officials from the Scandinavian countries.

APAP was established in 1993 by a group of young people, some of whom had legal training, as an organization dedicated to the promotion of public awareness about civil liberties and respect for the rule of law[17]. It is the second oldest human rights organization in the country after EHRCO. Among its many activities are informing the public about existing laws and legal institutions protecting the right of citizens. This is done through the distribution of booklets, posters, and articles in the newspapers. The basic assumption is that to disseminate legal knowledge among the public will help citizens be aware of their rights. Another activity centers on providing human rights training to

---

[17] The discussion is based on unpublished APAP documents

members of the judiciary as well as officers in the police force. This is meant to make law enforcement officers aware of the rights of citizens and detainees and to make the treatment of people under arrest or in detention better through respect for their rights. APAP has been conducting such training in various parts of the country for the last five years. A third important activity has been providing legal service in collaboration with the Ethiopian Bar Association. APAP has set up a legal service center to provide legal service to poor people who cannot afford to pay for lawyers. It also provides legal and other assistance to children and women who have been sexually abused. This is part of its defense of children and in particular children who have been forced into prostitution.

APAP was closed down in 1994 by the government on the grounds that it was carrying out work beyond the mandate for which it was established. It took nearly two years of persistent struggle by the organization before it was allowed to resume its activities.

The two human rights organizations that we shall examine closely are the Ethiopian Human Rights Council (EHRCO), and the Ethiopian Women Lawyers Association (EWLA). Both are membership organizations and both were established in the 1990s following the collapse of the Derg.

EHRCO, the first human rights organization in the country, was established in 1991. It is the only human rights organization which monitors human rights violations in the country and issues periodic reports on them[18]. These reports have had wide readership but they have angered the government which has disputed the reports' accusations claiming that they are based on false evidence and politically motivated.

The government tried to silence EHRCO from the early days of the organization but without much success. Initially it refused to approve the Council's application for registration alleging that EHRCO is a political organization and should be registered as such. A media campaign to brand the organization as an anti-government political movement and to discredit it in the eyes of the public in the mid-1990s backfired and may in fact have enhanced the stature of the organization. Later, the government decided to establish its human rights commission and ombudsman office to compete with EHRCO but the initiative has yet to bear fruit. In 1996, the state-owned Commercial Bank blocked EHRCO's account and the organization had to rely on public donations to cover its basic expenses and

---

[18] The discussion is based on EHRCO documents

71

maintain its activities. The Council sued the Bank but the court was reluctant to handle the case. International donors, no doubt pressured by the government, were unwilling to provide financial support or speak-up on its behalf. In mid-1999, EHRCO's application for registration was finally approved and its bank account was unblocked soon after. The move came as part of the government's effort to woo the voluntary sector following the war with Eritrea. Since its legal registration, the organization has become more active outside Addis Ababa and has been able to establish a number of branch offices in other parts of the country.

Many of the major diplomatic missions, including the U.S., were expressly unhappy with EHRCO. It is quite telling that Western donor agencies which placed so much emphasis on civil society as the best hope for fostering democratization in Africa felt it prudent to kowtow to the government when it decided to take punitive measures against the one and only human rights organization in the country.

While it is too early to judge at this point there is no evidence that EHRCO's efforts have had any impact on the process of law enforcement and the conduct of government authorities. EHRCO does not provide legal assistance to the public: it does not represent aggrieved persons in court nor offer legal advice or support to those who may seek it. It is on the strength of its reports and documentation that it hopes to achieve its main objectives. Due in part to government hostility and harassment, EHRCO's activity has been confined to Addis Ababa and its range of functions fairly limited.

EWLA was established in the mid-1990s by a group of women lawyers to defend women's rights through the legal system, to raise public awareness about the plight of women, and to agitate for reforms promoting gender equality[19]. Its main activities consist of legal aid to women, public education and advocacy for legal reforms, and research and documentation. The organization has three main branch offices outside Addis Ababa (in Assossa, Bahr Dar, and Nazret), and operates through eleven committees at the regional level, and twelve voluntary committees at the zonal and *woreda* levels distributed throughout the country. Committee members are given a short para-legal training and encouraged to take an active role in protecting women's rights in their localities.

The legal aid program, which is probably one of the most central of EWLA's activities, provides a wide variety of legal advice and counseling to women, including court representations by EWLA

---

[19] The discussion that follows is based on EWLA documents

lawyers. The service is offered free of charge to all that come seeking help. While the overwhelming majority of EWLA clients are women, a few men have also sought legal aid, not for themselves but on behalf of their female relatives. About 85 percent of the cases brought to EWLA involve marital conflict, and the rest consist of rape, abduction, robbery and theft, and assault and battery. Over 4000 women have received legal aid since EWLA began the program in 1996; most of the women were from poor and disadvantaged social backgrounds. Many of the women who came seeking EWLA support heard about the organization either through EWLA's public education program transmitted over the broadcast media, through word-of-mouth, or through the organization's advertising campaign. EWLA has had some notable successes in court and this has enhanced its stature among women. Many women are now aware that they can turn to EWLA if they feel they have been victims of gender-based injustice. In this respect, it is filling an important gap and providing an invaluable service

The main aim of the public education program, another important component of EWLA's activities, is to help bring about change in public attitudes towards women. The program consists of several activities carried out in the capital and the regions, including workshops and seminars involving law enforcement officials, judges, women and concerned individuals; educational material broadcast on radio which is particularly aimed at encouraging women's rights activists; and leaflets and posters. The program has been instrumental in gaining EWLA wide publicity and raising EWLA's profile especially among women who have been victims of marital injustice and gender discrimination. EWLA has also invested considerable effort in legislative reform. While the goal is to bring about the amendment of laws discriminating against women, the main focus so far has been on the reform of the Family Law which was enacted in 1960 during the imperial regime but which was still in the statute books until the second half of 2000. EWLA submitted a draft amendment of the Law to the federal and regional legislative bodies in 1996, but it was not until July 2000 that a new Family Law was finally enacted. While the organization did not succeed in getting all its recommendations accepted by Parliament, the new law that was passed by the legislature provides significant improvements on the earlier one (*Berchi* 2000). It is to the credit of EWLA that the reform of the Family Law became a public issue and that the government felt compelled to revisit the legislation. EWLA was also actively engaged in promoting women candidates in the parliamentary elections that took place in May 2000.

EWLA was placed under suspension and its activities were blocked in September 2001 by order of a senior government official, the Minister of Justice. The organization was in effect closed down although the Ministry's subsequent statements clarifying its decision made a distinction between suspension and closure. The reason given by the Ministry for its decision was neither justified nor legally defensible, but in view of the fact that the country's judiciary is not an independent institution but was subservient to the Ministry of Justice the organization was unable to get legal redress. It was the opinion of many that EWLA's activities in support of women's rights and the challenge it was posing to decision-makers in this regard was being looked at with a jaundiced eye by senior officials in government. EWLA is the most important human rights organization in the country fighting for women's rights, and to close it down was to strike a blow against women. EWLA remained closed for nearly two months despite the public outcry and the support it was gaining from civil society organizations and the media, both public and private. The suspension was finally lifted in October following a cabinet reshuffle and the appointment of a new Minister of Justice.

While some donor countries, in particular Norway, showed concern and raised the matter with government authorities, there was no concerted effort on the part of the larger donor community to convey its concern to the government regarding the unjust treatment of EWLA. EWLA receives financial support from a large number of donors, of which the following may be cited: a consortium or donors consisting of Norway, Netherlands, Sweden and Finland, and also Oxfam U.K and Canada, USAID, and the Friedrich Ebert Stiftung of Germany.

8. Conclusions

A number of international human rights groups have alleged that the response by some of the big donor countries, in particular the U.S., to gross human rights violations perpetrated by the government's security forces has been muted and disappointing (Human Rights Watch; Africa Watch). The significance of Ethiopia to the U.S war on terrorism has grown following the al-Qaeda attack on New York and the Pentagon in September 2001. Both rights organizations argue that Ethiopia has now become a partner and 'frontline state' in the war against international terrorism and the U.S. does not wish to antagonize the Ethiopian government over the issue of human rights. They point out that officials at the State Department in Washington and the U.S. Embassy in Addis Ababa indicated that the U. S. wields no leverage over Ethiopia, which is of course not entirely true. As noted above, the US continues to provide extensive humanitarian and development assistance, but it has not demanded accountability with regard to human rights. Human Rights Watch quotes 'a senior State Department official' as saying that the "the country's human rights record is 'not a factor' in the bilateral relations" between the two countries (Human Rights Watch: 42). Pausewang *et al.* argue that the U.S. has been apologetic about the country's human rights record. The U.S. Embassy in Addis Ababa has continued to insist that the new government "was better than the military dictatorship ... and having started from scratch, needed time to develop a more democratic society." America's aim of maintaining stability in the Horn of Africa, they note, has made it "overlook severe violations of human rights and excuse outright manipulation of elections ... ." (2002:43).

One of the authors of this report along with half a dozen heads of civil society organizations recently had an informal meeting with Mr Brian Goldbeck, the newly appointed counselor for Political and Economic Affairs at the U.S Embassy here in Addis Ababa[20]. Asked about the evident lack of active concern of the U.S regarding human rights and democratization issues in Ethiopia, Mr Goldbeck replied that his government was not down-playing the importance of these issues but had only adopted a different approach and was pursuing them with the Ethiopian authorities through informal channels, behind the scenes and without attracting publicity. He also stated that his government does not have a political problem with Ethiopia.

Human Rights Watch credits the European Union for demonstrating 'an increased willingness to take a stand on human rights violations in Ethiopia' in recent years (ibid: 43). In an interview we had with the political officer of the EC Delegation in Ethiopia, we were informed that the EU has formally taken a 'demarche', as he called it, on a number of human rights cases, requesting the government for an explanation concerning rights violations by security forces in the Awassa and Tepi incidents, and demanding an independent investigation of the matter. On the other hand, other donors have not taken any determined measures to hold the government accountable on cases of serious human rights violations. A few donors have made some effort to convey their concern to the

---

[20] Luncheon at Goldbeck's residence, 10 December 2003.

government but none have shown any willingness to take a public stand on abuses carried out by the security forces.

Thanks to the work of the half a dozen or so local human rights organizations, there is a relatively greater awareness of human rights issues among the public, at least among the urban public, on the one hand, and among the diverse set of civil society groups on the other. Many issues related to human rights are discussed in the private press, and drafts of government legislation are frequently scrutinized from the human rights point of view. Some human rights groups have prepared short briefs on the constitutional rights of citizens which they have distributed to the communities they work with as well as the wider public. Public education on human rights and the constitution has also been aired on the local FM radio.

There is some indication that the government is becoming somewhat more careful about human rights issues now than before. It is however still not willing to take measures against officials who have perpetrated serious human rights violations. In the Awassa case, a few local government officials were removed from their posts and this was taken by the donor community as a sign that the government is responding to donor pressure. But this is a minor measure compared to the scale of the violations. There are now government plans to provide human rights training to the police and other security forces as part of their basic training program but so far human rights training to these forces are undertaken by human rights groups only.

The following are more specific observations that the authors feel are important

- Donors only provide financial assistance, with some training and technical support on occasions. The initiative and ideas have come from local organizations or the government as the case may be.
- Financial assistance to human rights and other civil society organizations has important consequences: such organizations have been able to sustain their activities, to expand the scope and geographical reach of their work, and to reach more people and extend their influence.
- As a general rule donors have acted individually, and on occasions their individual interests have overridden their stated commitments to human rights. This has meant that they have not taken measures when they should have, in particular with regard to serious human rights violations by government security forces. The exception to this in respect of the Awassa and Tepi cases is the EU.

76

- Donor decisions may be influenced by personalities. Donor officials with a strong concern and active engagement have influenced decisions.
- OECD donors frequently operate in a consortium- the Human Rights Subgroup is responsible for human rights issues in the country. However, this body has no corporate identity and cannot make decisions or take measures on behalf of its members. It can only provide information to the members and it is up to o each member agency or country to take the appropriate measures. Donors we interviewed said this is a strength but we think it is a weakness.
- Donors' decisions and actions are inconsistent; there is no policy coherence. On some occasions donors have bowed to pressure from the government and have failed to take measures in support of human rights organizations: the harassment and/or closure of EHRCO, EWLA, and APAP was passed in silence or with only a few donor governments showing concern. Moreover, many of the big donors have declined to hold the government accountable for serious cases of human rights violations by the security forces.
- The government has made its own decision in some human rights cases against the interest of donors but there has not been any serious response from them. The case in point is the delay in the establishment of the Human Rights Commission and the Office of the Ombudsman about which it had made an initial commitment.

IV. THE MEDIA AND INTERNATIONAL ASSISTANCE

1. Introduction

Ethiopia's media has undergone dramatic change since the early 1990s following the fall of the military government and the establishment of the Transitional Government of Ethiopia (TGE). At the time of the Imperial and Derg regimes, the government was the sole owner of the means of public information and used the media to extend its power and legitimacy, to control the population, and to stifle public awareness. The Derg in particular employed the radio as a weapon of intimidation and terror: it was through radio broadcasts that the public heard about the execution of public officials, intellectuals, and political activists who were accused of sundry acts of sabotage and conspiracy against the "socialist revolution".

At the time of the Imperial regime, the media consisted, at first, of about a dozen state owned newspapers, and the national radio; television transmission began only in 1964. All print and broadcast media was owned by the state, except one independent monthly magazine, and a private radio station established in 1963 and operated by the World Lutheran Federation. The station's coverage of international news was comprehensive and of high standard but it exercised caution and self-censorship with regard to local news and programs. This was the only private broadcast media to have operated in the country to date; it was finally nationalized by the Derg following the Revolution. Under the Imperial regime, news, commentary and public affairs programs were heavily censored, and journalists and broadcasters could not express their views or report public opinion which in any way could be interpreted as being critical of the government or the Emperor. Censorship affected not just the media but all creative work as well.

One of the first acts of the Derg when it seized power was to ensure that the media was firmly under its control, and both it and the censor would serve the Revolution faithfully. The difference between the Derg and the Imperial regime in this regard was one of form only. While the latter believed press freedom did not exist except in the minds of the enemies of the country who were intent on destroying its 'Solomonic dynasty and Christian tradition', the Derg considered it as a bourgeois subterfuge and an imperialist tool designed against the socialist revolution. It was a little while before the media, especially the print media, which during the days before the Revolution had enjoyed a taste of freedom, was finally gagged by the Derg. Four independent monthly magazines were being published during the early, 'transitional' period of the Derg, but all four ceased publication by 1976 because the political environment was becoming prohibitive, and the threat of detention or worse was hanging over the editors and their staff.

The political context at the time of the change of government and the environment in which the deregulation of the press took place have had a lasting impact on the relation between the media and the government, and it may well be worth recapitulating briefly some of the major issues here. The political agenda of the new government when it seized power was to restructure the country's political, economic and social system along ethnic lines. Ethnic identity was to be the main criteria defining an individual and his or her relations with the state. Public employment, educational, economic and other opportunities, and political engagement were all to be based on ethnic criteria. The military, police and other security forces were also reorganized on the same basis. Pan-Ethiopian or issue-based political parties were not allowed to register since only ethnic parties were recognized. The end result was that the country's political landscape was radically changed and there was immense upheaval within the civil service and other public institutions in the first years of the transition

This chapter will discuss the institutional changes in the media brought about by the new government, the state of the media at present and the nature and impact of international assistance. As we shall try to show in the pages that follow, international assistance has had limited impact and the free press in particular continues to evolve primarily because of factors growing out of the present political context. Indeed, it may be said that international donor groups have, unwittingly, walked into a minefield the consequences of which have been counter-productive. A clear understanding of the context created in the post-conflict period is thus important

2. Context

a. Regulatory Framework

One of the first acts of the Transitional Government was to enact a press law, which deregulated the press, and which immediately had a dramatic impact on the country's media. While a small number of news magazines had started to appear soon after the fall of the Derg and before the press law was initiated, the deregulation of the print media allowing citizens or businesses to publish and distribute private newspapers, magazines, journals, periodicals and other news sources was accelerated by the new legislation. The legislation abolished censorship and allowed any Ethiopian citizen or group to carry on press activity provided that the person or group registers and obtains a license from the regulatory agency, the Ministry of Information or its Regional bureaus. Obtaining a license was made easy and simple, requiring only the submission of the names of the chief and deputy editors, the name of the press and the address of the publisher. The law also provided rights of access to information, in particular the right of the press to seek and obtain news and information from any branch of government (TGE 1992a). The allocation of radio waves to private investors was postponed for later legislation, which was finally issued in the form of the broadcast law of 1999. This law privatized the airwaves, allowing individuals and groups to own and operate private radio and television broadcast services (FDRE 1999). However, the implementation of this legislation and the privatization of the broadcast media has been delayed partly because the licensing agency was not established but more importantly because the government is apprehensive of losing one of its most important weapons of political control and manipulation.

There is broad agreement among informed opinion, and especially people in the media, that the press law of 1992 has opened the door to the growth of the private press in the country (see EFJA 2003; Mairegu 2003). The 1995 Constitution guarantees freedom of the press as well as of expression but there had been similar constitutions in the past but their impact on the media had been negligible. It was the press law which established the ground rules for the growth of the private press[21]. The immediate effect following the legislation was the proliferation of a wide diversity of newspapers, newsmagazines and other publications in Amharic and other local languages as well as in English. According to WAAG Communications (2003) the licensing department of the Ministry of Information has issued licenses for 182 magazines and 543 newspapers in the last ten years. At present, there are over 65 independent public affairs and general interest newspapers on the market, of which some 35 have been continuously published for five years or more. The number does not include newspapers specializing in sports, sex and religious matters. In addition, a large variety of

---

[21] For an extended discussion of the growth of the media and the private press since the early 1990s, see Shimelis 2000, 2002; Brook 2000.

commercial, cultural, and educational publications periodically flood the market. The end of censorship has also made it possible for civil society institutions, and in particular human rights and advocacy organizations to publish and freely distribute reports, studies, conference proceedings and public education materials.

The government still controls four national and at least five Regional newspapers as well as most of the broadcast media. A new development since the establishment of the present government is media ownership by the ruling party and its Regional affiliates. Media owned by the ruling parties includes one national and one Regional radio, and some seven newspapers. A few of the independent parties publish their own newspapers but these have very limited circulation. Table 4.1 below provides a brief picture of the state of the media in the country today.

Table 4.1 **Indicators of State of Media 2002**

Media	Govt Owned	Party Owned	Private	Community
Radio	1 National; 2 FM local; 1 Educational; 2 Regional	1 National; 1 Regional	None	None
TV	1 National; 1 Educational*	None	None	None
Newspapers	4 National; 5 Regional	7 by Govt Parties; 3 Ind.	65**	Unknown No.
News Service	1	1	None	None

Source: MoI 2002 and MoI Records; WAAG Communication 2003; Mairegu 2003; Brook 2000
*Note: * Transmitted through state TV.*
*   ** Not including sports and religious papers.*

b. Problems of the Media

Before we examine the problems of the media in greater depth, a brief discussion of the overall conditions facing the media is in order. By far the most important media in terms of its reach and impact is radio but due to poverty, and inadequate marketing and transport facilities, only a small percentage of the population listens to radio broadcasts, especially in the countryside. According to the last census, only 10 percent of rural households and 50 percent of urban households have radio sets. Television ownership is much smaller, and exclusively

81

restricted to urban households, of which a mere 7 percent were found to own TV sets (CSA 1999a). Radio Ethiopia, the government radio station, broadcasts in eight local languages, and in English, French and Arabic with a total broadcast time of 285 hours per week (MOI 2002). Its main news and current affairs program are broadcast in three of the country's main languages, namely Amharic, the official language of the country, and in Oromifa and Tigrigna. Discriminating listeners have access to foreign radio broadcasts but, according to a recent audience survey carried out in five major towns, these draw only a small percentage of the radio audience. The report found that half of the respondents in the survey were dissatisfied with Radio Ethiopia, and the main reasons given were bias and one-sidedness in news reporting, and the poor quality of other programs (Berhanu 2000).

Newspaper readership may be described as miniscule compared to the extent of the radio audience in the country, though there are no accurate figures available. According to the audience survey noted above, only 9 percent of respondents preferred newspapers as opposed to other media for news and information; the comparable figure for radio was 74 percent. Another recent survey of urban households found that 45 percent of respondents had never read a newspaper in their lives (Dessalegn and Aklilu 2002). Low newspaper readership is first and foremost a result of low literacy and low reading habits on the one hand, and poverty and low income on the other. Adult literacy rates in 1998 were 42 percent for males and 30 percent for females; the rates are lower in the rural areas. Secondly, most households cannot afford to buy newspapers on a regular basis especially when the papers do not provide any tangible benefit in return.

There are also other dimensions to the problem of the media in general. Unlike many other countries, the media in Ethiopia has no real impact on the lives of the great majority of the people. It does not provide reliable information, plays a very limited role in public education, and offers very little entertainment value (except to young people in the urban areas who find amusement in the music and soap opera broadcast on national or FM radio). In so far as the print media is concerned, almost all the papers published since the press law of 1992 are based in Addis Ababa, the capital, and reflect the narrow interests of the Addis Ababa literati. Moreover, many of the papers are not available outside the capital.

The private press is faced by a host of other problems: structural, economic, and professional. The fact that there is such a large number of papers on the market has meant stiff competition, limited sales and limited advertising revenue. According to information from the Ministry of Information, less than ten percent of the papers currently in publication have a circulation of 8,000 or more. Only a few papers, not more than five in number, have a circulation of over 10,000. As Table 4.2 below indicates, of the five main weekly papers shown only one newspaper derives good income from advertising. Advertising revenue is limited for many, and negligible for the majority. As Shimelis (2000) has shown, many press ventures are economically unviable and are operated under extremely difficult circumstances. Some papers are run on a shoestring budget and remain virtually one-man operations. Several papers have been able to survive only because they have been subsidized by 'patrons' of one sort or another (frequently exile political groups), or by donors and NGOs (see below). Over the last ten years, numerous papers have come and gone. According to WAAG Communications, 19 magazines and 74 newspapers have stopped publication for a variety of reasons over this period.

Table 4.2 **Sample of Five Independent Weekly Newspapers**

Name of Paper	Circulation	Av. No. of Pages	Av Advert. Space (%)
Addis Admas	29,000	20	18
Addis Zena	5200	24	16
Menelik	8000	16	14
Reporter (Amharic)	18,500	32	45
Tobya	5200	20	18

Source: MOI Records; recent issues of the newspapers. Circulation figures are
   actually number of print runs of each paper and are given by MoI as of June
   2003.

Moreover, the quality and level of professionalism of the private press has been a source of concern to the many readers, friends of press freedom as well as donors. Many of the papers show the worst excesses of yellow journalism. A recent statement by the Ethiopian Free Press Journalists Association (EFJA), the main organization for employees in the independent press, makes a number of significant criticisms of the free press. There is, it says, lack of professional ethics in reporting and news management. Often, stories are written without any evidence and without sufficient information. There is alarmist reporting, and reporting that is completely false. News reports often tell only one side of the story and provide no balance at all. Many of the papers suffer from a lack of professionally trained staff. There are not many trained journalist working for the private press; in fact in some cases, papers are managed by people who have very limited formal education. Financing is another major problem raised by the EFJA: many of the papers are not profitable and the need to economize severely hampers news gathering and report writing. There is, finally, a lack of cooperation and goodwill among free press journalists and between the free press and the government press (EFJA 2003). Interestingly enough, unlike some countries, sex and violence have limited sales value in this country. On the contrary, what the city's literati find exciting is political sensationalism: the rise, fall or defection of officials within the ruling elite, conflict among them, embezzlement of public funds and the like.

The Prime Minister on one occasion described the private press as the 'gutter press'. To be fair to the press, we should note that the picture is a bit more complicated. While it is true that many of the papers that appeared with deregulation (and still appear today) were awful, some were better and making efforts to maintain a respectable standard. There has been a good deal of improvement over the years, and a small number of papers have grown to win public confidence. Survival in the marketplace has become tougher, readers have become more discriminating, and sensationalism no longer sells papers. For these reasons, and, paradoxically because of government pressure, the quality of newspaper production as well as journalism has improved to some extent. The report prepared by EJPA noted earlier states that despite the many weaknesses and constraints, the private press has established its identity and achieved a lot. The private press has a better record than the heavily subsidized government press in terms of public education; it has established a track record in investigative reporting, exposing policy failures, and inefficiency and corruption in public office. It has, the report goes on to note, been better able to present the diversity of views within society, and is beginning to serve as a 'watch dog' on behalf of the public interest (EFJA 2003). There is a good deal of truth in this assessment.

It is interesting to note that the proliferation of the private press and the competition created as a result has brought about some improvement in the state owned media as well. The public media now reports on inefficiency and malpractice in government agencies, and has offered debates in which critics of the government have participated. Occasionally, it reports on the activities of opposition political parties. This would have been unthinkable some ten years ago. Moreover, civil society organizations can now buy airtime on FM

Radio Addis, a recently established FM radio station owned by the government, and transmit their own programs. A number of human rights groups, policy research institutes, and the Ethiopian Chamber of Commerce have taken advantage of this opening to run public education programs over the last three years.

c. Relations between the Media and Government

From the very beginning relations between the independent press and the new government were on a collision course. The new government did not preach reconciliation soon after it seized power, on the contrary, government propaganda was inflammatory, and the state media was used to fan the flames of ethnic conflict. Ethnic politics was strongly resented by a large section of public opinion, especially in the urban centers. Ethiopian towns are an ethnic 'melting pot' containing people with diverse cultural and religious backgrounds living together, if not in harmony, at least tolerant of each other. Ethnic politics was now seen as a threat undermining the goals of what informed opinion would call unity within cultural diversity. Moreover, the new government, flushed with its victory over the Derg and its huge but feeble military apparatus was in no mood to enter into dialogue with any group or party over any issue. In short, reconciliation and dialogue were not part of the government's lexicon.

The independent press on its part was equally aggressive. A great majority of the papers that were launched following the deregulation was strongly critical of the new government. Indeed, quite a number of them were established for the main purpose of attacking the government and exposing the failings of ethnic politics. Of the 65 independent papers that are published at present less than five percent may be described as being sympathetic to the government. To many in the emerging press, and to a good section of urban public opinion, the new government was a minority government, dominated as it was by the Tigrian-based TPLF, and hence illegitimate. Pan-Ethiopianists believed the government had brought disrepute to the country and its long history and culture.

The conflict between the state and the press was thus deep rooted, and continued to grow as the government's ethnic program came to infuse many aspects of public and private discourse and as the improvements in the economy, in particular in the poverty situation, and in governance and administrative efficiency failed to materialize. There have been several costly government blunders, of which the Ethio-Eritrean relations leading to the war, the peace process, and the circumstances surrounding the decision by the Eritrea-Ethiopia Border Commission are some of the worst, which provided ammunition to the press. Under these circumstances, any donor initiative to promote dialogue or reconciliation in whatever sphere is bound to fall on deaf ears.

A persistent problem facing the free press is government discrimination and harassment. There is open and deliberate discrimination of the free press by the government which has taken the form of refusing to give information to it and not inviting any of the papers for press conferences or news worthy official events. While the 1992 legislation acknowledges the right to information and states that the press has a right to information from government agencies, this is denied in reality. The press conferences given by the Prime Minister in the last ten years have always excluded the free press. The government media and that of the ruling party are given preferential treatment. Even donors were initially reluctant to provide information and news releases to the private press. This has contributed to poor journalism in the free press, for in the absence of news, journalist have turned to the city's active rumor mill and have even occasionally made their own, often sensational stories. There has been some change in the last few years, and some government agencies are now beginning to make an opening and provide information to a select number of private newspapers.

The threat to press freedom posed by government hostility to the private press has been a serious one for quite some time and still remains a danger. The harassment and victimization of independent journalists has taken a toll, and while the number of victims and the frequency of harassment have decreased over the years, it cannot be assumed to be a thing of the past. Table 4.3 shows the number of journalists that were victims of government harassment in 1994 as reported by EHRCO; no comparable figures are available for later years.

Table 4.3 **Threats to Press Freedom 1994**

Measures Against Journalists	No of Journalists
Detention without charge	2
Sentenced 6-24 months in prison	7
Fined (varying amounts of money)	13
Released on bail	21
On appeal or in litigation	15
Suspended jail sentence (12-18 months)	6
Acquitted by court	9

Source: Based on EHRCO 1999: 124.

Since the 1994 report, EHRCO has reported on the detention and harassment of four journalists working for the weekly paper *Tobya* which occurred in 1996. The journalists were detained without charge for various lengths of time and released on bail. The same journalists were again arrested in 1998 charged with printing material threatening the peace of the country. While they were in detention the paper's office was burnt down in mysterious circumstances, and because of that and the arrest of the staff the paper ceased publication for four months. EHRCO has also reported the cases of several journalists subjected to harassment and detention in 2001 (EHRCO 2003: 196 ff). According to the report, the editor of *Tomar*, another weekly paper, was arrested for publishing a report on inter-ethnic conflict in one of the Regions. He was held without charge for several weeks and later released. The report also describes threats and harassment of editors and journalists on three other newspapers. According to the head of the EFJA, there have been some 200 journalists put in detention, some more than once, in the last five years. About 35 to 38 face legal cases pending in the courts[22].

The recent decision by the government to draft a new press law to replace the law of 1992 has been interpreted by many, including the independent media as well as civil society organizations as an attempt to muzzle the media, and in particular the country's fledgling private press. The draft legislation is highly restrictive in terms of access to information, reporting, financing and newspaper distribution. There have been numerous articles in the private press criticizing the draft law and calling for significant revisions. EFJA has taken a very active role in defending the rights of the free press and expressing its

---

[22] Interview with Kifle Mulat, President of EFJA

opposition to the new law. Civil society organizations have also expressed their concern: a free press is of central importance to the work and growth of civil society and the draft law poses a threat to press freedom. Attempts to promote dialogue on the issue between the government and the private media, which took the form of a number of public conferences, some of which financed by donors such as the EU, DFID and the Austrian Embassy, have not been successful. The government has refused to make any compromise and the press has understandably been sharp in its criticism. The international free press movement as well as African press organizations have sent strong messages of support to the EFJA and of protest to the government. Despite the public outcry, the draft legislation has been submitted to the Council of Ministers, the first step on its way to Parliament.

3. International Assistance

International assistance to the media (both public as well as private) has been limited in scope, and relatively insignificant in terms of its impact. International donors have failed to make a strategic intervention in the media sector and have been limited to low level support with only limited results. The following have been the main forms of assistance provided.

a. International Assistance to Media for Elections.

Both the electoral law of 1993 and the broadcast legislation of 1999 stipulate that candidates- both individuals and political organizations-contesting elections are entitled to equal and free access to the public media. However, it is not easy to monitor whether or not these laws have been fully implemented. Candidates have to request access to the media but not all candidates were aware during the last elections that they were entitled to this right. Nevertheless, the findings of one study show that the free air time allotted for the 2000 elections was used mostly by independent opposition candidates; only three opposition political organizations out of a total of 50 took advantage of their media access rights (Berhanu and Meleskachew 2001). The study goes on to show that government candidates in contrast made maximum and more effective use of the free airtime allotted to them. Polhemus (2002) states that one of the "improvements in the 2000 elections was greater and more systematic access to the state owned media for the opposition than there had been previously" but many opposition groups did "not make optimal use of the access they did gain." There has been very little donor support to the government media targeted to election coverage.

The picture is quite different and complicated when it comes to the private press. Elections do not make hot news nor do they sell newspapers, at least not in this country. During the last elections, none of the candidates on either side of the political divide had a media personality, and none of them offered ideas, programs or visions that excited the public imagination. In fact, Ethiopia's elections have been tedious affairs: dull campaigns, limited news-worthy events, and lack of media savvy among most of the campaigners. There has also been widespread public opinion, shared by many in the press, that the outcome of the elections was a foregone conclusion, and that there was no level playing field in the contest. Hence many papers were not keen to provide wide coverage. Important events during the campaign were reported and the press conferences called by the opposition groups were given coverage but otherwise the coverage in the private media was fairly limited. On the other hand, scandals and malpractices related to the elections have been eagerly seized upon by it.

Donor assistance to the private press in this regard has been restricted to training of journalists (including government media journalists) on election coverage, and financial support to selected newspapers to publish articles related to voter education, and to provide expanded coverage of the campaigns of opposition candidates. Opposition candidates had limited resources to spend on media exposure, and whatever funds were spent on advertising by them went to state radio and television because these reach a wider public than newspapers, public or private. The private press did not benefit commercially during the elections except in the form of donor financial support.

b. International Assistance for Training of Journalists.

There have been numerous programs initiated and/or supported by a large number of donors to provide skills training to journalists in the last ten years. Most of these have been short programs, ranging from half a day to a week, in which trainers brought from outside (on occasions, local trainers) have given lectures on the basic skills of the profession. Almost all of the major donors in the country have supported one or more programs of this kind at one time or another. The programs are given free to journalists working for the private or government media, nevertheless, how well attended they are depends on whether or not trainees are paid to attend the programs. The instructions are often given in English, but a majority of the trainees do not use English in their work, and have very limited understanding of the language. There are only a small number of English language newspapers published in the country.

Many veteran journalists, some of whom have been involved in the training program as trainers or resource persons, are very dissatisfied with the program provided by donors. There is no coordination or continuity in the programs: each training program is new, involving new trainers and new trainees. The selection of trainees is random, and frequently the wrong person attends the programs. Moreover, trainers from abroad do not understand the reality facing local journalists, and thus the training is often not relevant to their needs[23]. Except for one or two courses in journalism offered at Addis Ababa University, and of late at Unity College, a private college in the capital, there is no school of journalism in the country to train journalists. The government's Mass Media Training Institute (MMTI), which was established at the end of 1996 is the only institution which provides professional training and offers a diploma in journalism. However, as a government body, its programs are open to journalists working in the government media and media operated by the ruling parties (Brook 2000). No keen interest has been shown on the part of the private media to take advantage of the opportunities offered by it. According to a senior official at the Institute, journalists from the private press are welcome to enroll as trainees but the response has not been encouraging[24]. For these reasons, not many donors have shown interest in supporting the Institute.

c. Other Support to the Private Press.

Selected newspapers have benefited from what for lack of a better term we have called financial 'subsidy' by donors and NGOs. Such 'subsidy' takes the form of payment to one or more newspapers to publish articles on a specific subject to serve as a means of public education. Donors or NGOs with particular interest on a particular issue of public concern will pay a newspaper to publish articles on such subjects either prepared by themselves or by the newspaper itself. Some of the issues on which papers have run public education articles include HIV/AIDS, the environment, human rights, violence against women, pastoralism, as well as media professional ethics.

---

[23] Iinterview with Teferi Wossen, WAAG Communications.
[24] Interview with Ammanuel Abdissa of MMTI

Sometimes, however, the choice of newspapers to support in this manner has been made on inadequate criteria and reflects a lack of hard-headedness or sound judgment.

d. Assistance to Regulatory Reforms.

As was noted above, the main alternative media in the country so far is the private press, and this media was up and running long before international assistance programs were on offer. One area which has raised keen interest among some donors is the deregulation of the electronic media. Ethiopia must be one of the few African countries which has not allowed private radio and television. The broadcast legislation of 1999 established the ground rules for the licensing of private radio and television and there was hope among many that the entry of the private sector into the electronic media would be allowed soon. However, this has been a big disappointment to the public, the private sector as well as donors because the government is dragging its feet and continuing to delay the implementation of the legislation. A number of business interests have drawn up plans and invested resources in preparation for the privatization of the airwaves but they have been frustrated by the delay. Donors such as Norway and foreign broadcast organizations such as the BBC have invested time and money to help local media interests prepare for the day of privatization.

The government is apprehensive that private radio and television will undermine its monopoly on the airwaves as well as its political power. The Broadcast Agency, which is mandated to issue licenses, monitor and regulate radio and TV transmission, has been in business for over a year but so far no licenses have been issued. In an interview with the deputy manager of the Agency, we asked why the licensing process has been delayed for so long. The official's response was that the Agency has not yet been able to employ trained staff capable of carrying out the tasks entrusted to it by the legislation. At the moment, he said, the Agency has filled only 60 percent of its staff needs. He pointed out also that the Agency does not yet have enough technical capability to regulate private broadcasters. He went on to note that there are inconsistencies between the broadcast law and the newly drafted press legislation and these need to be ironed out before licenses are issued[25]. The Agency has not so far been a beneficiary of international assistance. Several donors, among which Norway, the

---

[25] Interview with Desta Tesfaye

Netherlands and DFID may be cited, have shown keen interest in the deregulation of the broadcast media and have from time to time raised concerns to the government over the delay in issuing licenses.

On the other hand, donor support to enabling media legislation has been limited. The government is in the process of finalizing a draft freedom of information legislation, the background work for which was prepared by international consultants paid for by donors. As noted above, the controversial press law that has finally been submitted to the Council of Ministers was the work of the government alone, and apart from paying for some conferences to discuss the draft legislation and to try to promote dialogue between the press and the government, donors have had no hand in its content. It should be noted that not many donors have shown concern about the draft law, at least not in public, and this is surprising considering the fact that both the private press and public opinion believe that should the draft be finally approved and become law, the government will have struck a savage blow against press freedom.

e. Support to Media Organizations

Unlike many African countries, media organizations in Ethiopia are few in number. According to a recent study of broadcasting in Eastern Africa, for instance, there were more than a dozen journalists' associations in Kenya in 2000 (Wanyeki 2000), whereas in Ethiopia there are only two associations serving journalists, of which one is very inactive. Obviously the reason for this poor record has been the underdevelopment of the media, and the fact that until some ten years ago the media was a government monopoly. Even after deregulation, the hostility of the government to the private press has impeded progress and professional development.

The two associations that exist at present are the Ethiopian Free Press Journalists Association (EFJA) and the Ethiopian Media Women's Association (EMWA)[26]. The latter organization which was legally established in 1999, and whose aim is to promote the interest of women working in the media, is in the process of defining its role and has thus not been actively engaged. It has held a few workshops and published about two issues of its newsletter but so far it has not taken up any public programs or advocacy initiatives to pursue its objectives. It was established thanks mainly to the support it received

---

[26] There is an association for journalists working for the government media but the organization has been inactive for many years.

initially from the Netherlands Embassy. EFJA[27] was set up in 1992, following the deregulation of the media, however, according to the president of the Association, because of the hostility of the government, it has taken nearly ten years to get it registered under the law. Despite the pressure from government on the Association and the free press in general, the organization was kept running by a small number of dedicated members. In this country, it is extremely difficult to function as a civil society organization without registration. The organization cannot open a bank account and receive funds from donors if it is not legally registered.

EFJA is a membership organization; membership is open to those who are engaged in the private media. Journalists working for the state owned media do not have their own association because they have been prohibited from establishing one by their employer. At present, EFJA has 166 members and membership is growing especially in the last two to three years due to some easing of government pressure on the press following the Ethio-Eritrean war. The Association is still in the process of building its own competence, and some of the duties of its office are carried out by voluntary work; each member is expected to contribute one day of work a week to the Association. The decision-making structure consists of the general assembly of members which appoints the Executive Committee which carries out the decisions and policies made by the assembly. The president is the head of the Executive.

EFJA's major source of financial support has been the international free press movement. The Vienna based International Press Institute (IPI), and the International Freedom of Expression and Exchange (IFEX) have been its main source of funds so far. The organization is a member of IPI and has benefited a good deal because of that. Other international press organizations, including the London based PEN International, ARTICLE 19, and a number of Africa-based associations have offered moral support. Unfortunately, while they have shown a good deal of interest about the Association, donors based in the country have not offered any financial support to it.

EFJA's main responsibility, broadly speaking, is to promote the growth of the free press in the country and to defend press freedom. While it has not had sufficient clout, it has attempted to support

---

[27] Based on EFJA 2003, unpublished documents, and interview with Kifle Mulate, president of EFJA. In November 2003, the organization was suspended by the government, allegedly for failing to renew its registration. The suspension has been contested by the organization; international press organizations have sent protests to the government over its decision.

members who have been harassed or put in detention on account of what they have written or published in their papers. The Association, through its international connections, campaigns on behalf of journalists persecuted by the government. The other dimension of its responsibility is to promote the quality of journalism in the country. In this endeavor it has drafted a code of professional ethics for members and has held public discussions on it. It is keen to improve the management, design and marketing of newspapers in the private sector.

EFJA took a very active role in the recent campaign against the government's draft press law. As noted above, the new press law created a public outcry, and the feeble attempt to create dialogue by donors between the government and the press quickly flopped. The Association made a detailed criticism of the draft law, and drafted an alternative press law which it presented to the government for discussion. EFJA has frequently argued that the government's approach to the free press has been punitive and restrictive; the state has used the threat of punishment to control press activity. A better alternative, according to it, would have been constructive engagement which would have benefited the press and, at the same time, addressed the main concerns of the government.

EFJA has also criticized the government for restricting investment in the private media and is unhappy with the long delay in the implementation of the 1999 broadcast law and in the licensing of private radio and television as promised by the legislation. A bone of contention in the draft law between the government on the other hand and the independent press on the other is whether the government has a mandate to establish a Press Council. The new draft states that the government shall establish such a Council, but the argument of EFJA and the private press in general is that it is people in the profession who should create a Press Council which will be accountable to them. The Association has drafted a proposal for the establishment of an independent Press Council which is now being discussed among its members[28].

4. Impact of International Assistance

To begin with, the level of international financial and technical assistance to the media has been relatively small. Consequently, the

---

[28] Since these lines were written, the organization's leadership has been removed by the government and replaced by a new one.

impact of donor assistance on the media, in particular in terms of the progress made by the independent press, has been by and large quite limited. The state of the media in the country today, including that of the free press, has been largely a product of its own making and the consequence of domestic political, social and economic processes. Individual initiative, public choice, competition and market forces, together with state action have been responsible for the achievements and failures of the media in general and the private press in particular.

Donor assistance has mostly been concentrated on training programs for journalists; such programs have included visits arranged for journalist to foreign countries, and exchange of experiences among media people in the Horn of Africa. Assistance has also taken the form of financial support to selected newspapers to publish articles on the elections and other issues. And finally, international press organizations such as the International Press Institute, International Freedom of Expression and Exchange and others have provided financial assistance to EFJA as well as moral support to the cause of press freedom in Ethiopia. Both Amnesty International and Africa Human Rights Watch have reported on the arrest, detention and harassment of journalists on many occasions.

Donor support has been provided without a clear understanding of the realities facing the media in the country. In the first place, as few donor staff speak or read Amharic or other local languages -the main languages of the media- their views of the state of the media have been shaped by the small number of English language papers that are published and the limited English programs broadcast on the electronic media. The English language media is a poor reflection of media in the country. There has been a tendency on the part of the donor community to offer support which is either not quite relevant or inadequate. Moreover, the type of assistance that has commonly been offered has largely been 'short-termist', that is, it is oriented towards short-term outcomes. Long-term investment in institution and capacity building has not been given serious consideration. Let us look closely at the some of the main support offered by donors.

While accurate figures are not available, training of journalists has been the area where donors have invested considerably. There have been numerous training programs sponsored by donors but without coordination or follow up. The assumption behind these programs has been that if only media people were given some crash courses in the basics of their profession, the quality of journalism would markedly improve. But the problem is much more complicated than that. It is true that journalists need more training but this is not the main reason why the quality of reporting and news management is in such a poor state in the country. Journalists in the public sector cannot operate freely or in accordance with professional standards because their employer makes heavy demands on them. Journalists in the private sector are driven in part by stiff competition and in part because the papers they work on have definite political agendas. Equally significant has been the fact that the free press has been denied access to information by the government and is routinely excluded from all official press conferences. Moreover, the journalists that come to participate in the training programs are not the ones who make the important decisions: they do not have the power to initiate changes in standard, quality or style.

More significantly, short-term training is not what is needed. The training given by each program is different with different instructors and different participants. We have also noted earlier that there is a language problem (the instructors do not speak the local language and the trainees have a poor grasp of English), that the instruction given is frequently not relevant to the needs of the trainees, and that on occasions the wrong people are selected. In brief, the investment in training programs is wasted investment. What is needed is long-term investment on an institution (or institutions) and on capacity building. The establishment of an independent school of journalism to train journalist for the public and private sector is one such sound investment. There are now plans to establish a school of journalism at Addis Ababa University supported by NORAD, the Norwegian aid agency. This is a positive step and should have been considered long ago. The Mass Media Training Institute, noted above, is a government institution and while there is no express discrimination against the private sector, journalists in the sector do not have confidence in it and have not shown any interest in enrolling in it. Another option is to invest in civil society institutions working with journalists, such as for example EFJA, to build up capacity so that they become responsible for promoting professional and responsible conduct among journalists.

Donor support to election coverage may be faulted along similar lines. Until electioneering becomes relevant and interesting to the public and until the opposition candidates learn to make sound and creative use of the media, the press will find it difficult to devote space to elections, which in the past have been dull and uninspiring. Even with improvements in the campaign process, the main beneficiaries with be the electronic media and not the private press for obvious reasons. Moreover, it should be the candidates and political parties who should decide which media outlet and which newspaper will serve their purposes best.

Regarding indirect subsidies to the press, several important issues need to be carefully considered. To begin with, the practice of paying newspapers to publish public education material is not a sound decision. This has helped some struggling newspapers to stay afloat when the public interest would have best been served if they were left to close down. Donors, in other words, have made interventions which has prevented the normal workings of the market place. Secondly, on occasions the choice of which newspaper to 'subsidize' has been made on poor criteria or without adequate knowledge and thus the "wrong" papers have been supported. There are far too many papers being published at present. Almost all the papers are based in the capital, and except for a few, do not have a market outside the city. The purchasing power of the city's residents cannot sustain more than a handful. Many of the major cities in Europe or North America do not maintain more than half a dozen or so papers, but the market here is literally over-flooded with newspapers and news magazines. One of the reasons for the poor quality of the press has to do with this fact. Thus, subsidizing papers serves no useful purpose, and instead one should adopt a hard-headed approach.

In so far as enabling legislation is concerned, the record of international donors in this regard leaves a lot to be desired. The first order of business here is to make the government understand that donors are strongly committed to press freedom, and they should express strong concern when there are threats to press freedom on the part of the government. This has, by and large, been lacking among donors in this country. A good example is donor response to the restrictive press law drafted by the government recently. The donor's sub-committee on the press, which is a subcommittee of the Human Rights Subgroup, did discuss the matter at a few of its meetings but since it does not have the power to make decisions, it was only able to pass on information about the law to the donor embassies concerned. Some donors, such as for example the Netherlands and Norwegian Embassies, did express their concern to the government through their Ambassadors; however, they were not actively supported by many donors which have more leverage over the government. The media has not been given as much attention by donors as other elements of the democratization process.

In so far as support to civil society organizations working with the media are concerned, it is disappointing to note that donors have not made serious efforts to support EFJA, the main professional association for journalists in the country. The Association has survived thanks to the support it has received from a number of international press organizations and the support of its members[29].

---

[29] These lines were written before the suspension of the Organization.

V. CONCLUSIONS

In this chapter, we shall try to present the main findings of our study and point to some of the major issues that have a bearing on the impact of democratic assistance. These issues may be taken as broad recommendations to donors and others, however, we hope they will be used as a starting point for further debate rather than as a blueprint for change.

Limitations of Democratic Assistance

As the discussion in the preceding chapters has shown, donor assistance to the democratization process in Ethiopia has been comparatively limited. In contrast, donors have invested heavily in the humanitarian and relief effort on the one hand, and in the socio-economic development sectors on the other. Assistance to both sectors has been growing in the last ten years, and in particular assistance to the humanitarian sector has been increasing markedly in this period. Indeed, donor assistance in support of food security has been going on since the second half of the 1970s. By all standards, donor support to the electoral process has been fairly significant while support to the media has been relatively low.

On the other hand, financial support to civil society, especially local human rights and advocacy organizations, has been instrumental in enabling the growth of the voluntary sector in the country. Without such support, civil society would have faced more difficult and trying circumstances, and its achievements, especially in the areas of human rights monitoring, training and advocacy would have been far more limited. However, to put the matter in perspective, we should note that the dependence of civil society organizations on donor funding is not unique to Ethiopia. Many of the global advocacy organizations, such as, for example, Amnesty International, Human Rights Watch, Oxfam International, Greenpeace, etc. depend on donor funding for most of their program activities.

An important finding of our study is that the impact of international assistance on the democratization process in this country has been very limited in terms of enduring results. The successes registered to date in the areas of elections, human rights and press freedom have primarily been a product of local initiative, local organizations, struggles by stakeholders, and an increasingly complex political reality to which the government has had to respond. International assistance has of course provided the resources that enabled civil society, the democratic stakeholders and the government to take important initiatives and to respond to emerging realities.

On the other hand, the following are some of the major limitations of democratic assistance and the structural weaknesses of donor-government relations. The list is not meant to be exhaustive but reflects what we believe to be important ones that need to be debated and addressed.

To begin with, donors rarely speak with one voice, and except for electoral support, assistance programs on democratization and governance are not offered in a well-coordinated manner among them. Donors speak with one voice when they wish to do so, and a few examples may illustrate this point. There was near unanimity among donors during the Ethio-Eritrean war: they supported Eritrea and criticized Ethiopia, and froze all development assistance to the country until the peace treaty was signed in December 2000. Most donors have insisted that Ethiopia should accept the IMF-World Bank's structural adjustment program to reform its economy. Finally, many donors have adopted what is known as direct budget support (DBS) switching from their previous project approach. Here, donors channel their aid directly to the state treasury for the government to use in accordance with its plans and priorities. The government is obliged to provide to donors progress reports based on a broad set of indicators. While this may make it easy for the government to plan and implement program activities, there is concern that DBS will strengthen the government bureaucracy and reinforce the dominance of the ruling party. It will in the long run undermine democratic change by making the government accountable to the donor community only and not to its own citizens.

Moreover, decisions by donors with regard to human rights issues, issues of press freedom and responses to government failings in these areas are frequently inadequate and do not inspire confidence that the donor community is serious about promoting democratization and good governance in the country. The working consortia formed by different groups of donors, such as the Human Rights Subgroup, or ad hoc groupings set up to support the election process during elections are by and large forums for discussion and information exchange. Such consortia do not have a corporate body, i.e. they do not have the power to make decisions on behalf of their members but only to provide information. The European Union is the exception in this regard: it can make decisions and take measures once a common agreement is reached by all member countries. However, the EU's decision-making process is cumbersome and very time consuming, and the decisions that are finally arrived at will have been substantially revised (and watered down) from the original version in order to accommodate every member's wishes.

Secondly, there are many forums in which either donors by themselves or donors and government officials meet regularly to discuss economic, political and other issues. There are, on the other hand, no similar forums where citizens' voices and the voices of civil society are heard. The donors-only forums include the OECD Ambassadors Group, and the Development Assistance Group (DAG) which meets monthly; the DAG consists of all donors represented in the country. Then there is the Government-Donor Coordinating Meetings which are a forum for both. The only forum where a few NGOs have been allowed to participate (mainly because of their HIV/AIDS programs) is the Sector Development Group which brings together government, donors and NGOs (see UNDP 2001 for other coordination groups). This arrangement tends to foster dialogue between donor and government only, with the result that the government feels it is accountable to the donor community and not to its citizens. Such framework does not give importance to dialogue with and accountability to citizens' groups by either the government or donors. This does not foster responsible governance and democratic principles. It tends to not only marginalize non-state actors but also to send out the wrong signals to civil society and the public at large. This needs to be changed to allow tripartite dialogue involving government, donors and civil society.

Thirdly, few donors have sufficient leverage over the government to hold it accountable if and when there are failings on its part or if government actions violate democratic principles. The donor group may be divided into three parts: a) the great major of donors which provide, individually, a small percentage of the total assistance fund to the country; b) donors which are part of the UN system, or include the Bretton Woods institutions; c) a small number of donors whose assistance makes up a substantial portion of total assistance to the country. The first have limited leverage over the government. For instance both the Netherlands Embassy and the Norwegian Embassy provide about 5 percent each of the total assistance; the U.K provides much less. When acting individually, such countries do not have sufficient leverage to put pressure on the government on any substantive issue. Among the Bretton Woods institutions, the World Bank provides a substantial percentage of the assistance to the country; however, the Bank's support goes primarily to socio-economic development, and as a consequence it tends to project a low profile in matters having to do with governance and democratization.

Donors within the UN system do not make coordinated decisions nor do they harmonize their activities. Each donor in this group is a small actor in terms of its impact on the government or the country's needs.

The exception to all this is the United States and the European Union. The US is by far the largest donor in all categories of assistance and thus the only country with potentially a preponderant power to influence the decisions of the Ethiopian government. The EU is also an important provider of assistance; if we add to this, the assistance provided individually by the member countries, the EU's influence can come to rival that of the US. Moreover, the EU is the largest provider of food aid to the country and food aid has come to be the Achilles heel of the Ethiopian government. What this means is that a majority of donors do not have sufficient power to influence the pace or conditions of democratization in the country.

Fourthly, international assistance is not often free of politics. Each donor is driven by the national interest of its own government. Moreover, the dynamics of geopolitics, the desire to promote stability and peace in the Horn of Africa, and the war on international terrorism, have led big donors such as the United States to "befriend" the Ethiopian government, to refrain from raising issues of democratic performance and to decline to use their influence on matters of importance to the democratization process.

Fifthly, the Ethiopian experience suggests that international electoral assistance, given in an environment characterized by chaos and poor organization of the electoral process, will not be effective in promoting democratic elections. Aid given under such an environment can be wasted or abused, and it is extremely difficult to provide full accounting on its use. The absence of effective monitoring and follow up has meant that a full assessment of the impact cannot be undertaken and best practices that can be replicated elsewhere are not documented. Moreover, donors have not given sufficient emphasis to the need to build up local capacity for monitoring elections. Sooner or later this country must rely on its own ability to monitor elections and to oversee the democratic process. International monitors, while important in providing international expertise and comparability, do not often have adequate knowledge of the complexity of the national political landscape.

Sixthly, international assistance will be more effective if it is institutionalized and objectives and targets are clearly spelt out. International assistance for institutional and judicial reform to Ethiopia can be cited as a good example in this case. Reports were produced on time and distributed to all the parties to the project.

Results were easily measurable and monitorable. Effective follow up of progress and lack of it were made easy. As a result, impact assessment was made less difficult and the strengths of the project could be identified to be experimented elsewhere under similar circumstances.

Seventhly, democratization and the culture of good governance are long-term processes and cannot be achieved overnight. International assistance has frequently invested in projects or activities which show quick results when what is required is investing in the long term. Indeed, it will not be unfair to say that "short-termism" characterizes many aspects of donor assistance. The short-term approach may be seductive but will not have lasting value. Building institutions, in particular human rights, advocacy and other civil society institutions, and enhancing capacity in existing institutions have not received the importance they deserve by many donors. The disproportionate focus on elections rather than wider democratization issues has not advanced the democratic process. Moreover, related to this is the failure of donor assistance to make a strategic intervention, i.e. interventions with long-term and multiple benefits, in the areas of elections, human rights and the media.

Lastly, in many instances, donors have made decisions without sufficient understanding of the country, its needs and the dynamics of democratization. As has been noted in the preceding chapters, donors have not had sufficient understanding of the dynamics having to do with the electoral process, human rights and the media in the country. Quite often, donors are interested in promoting programs that are currently in vogue and that have been designed without taking into account the specific realities of the country. Such programs come with pre-conceived assumptions. A point related to this is that on occasions dynamic and proactive donor personalities have had a significant impact on programs and relations between donors and the government. However, the frequent turnover of donor staff has had a damaging impact on continuity and sustainability. Many of the donor staff we interviewed for this study had been on their post from a few months to a year, and the experienced staff had been transferred to other countries. This involves a considerable loss of local knowledge and expertise in managing aid and monitoring progress.

REFERENCES

[*NOTE*: Following customary usage, Ethiopian authors are listed by first name.]

Abbink, Jon 2000 (Eds). The Organization and Observation of Elections in Federal Ethiopia: Retrospect and Prospect. In Abbink, Jon and Hesseling, Gerti. **Election Observation and Democratization in Africa**. New York: St. Martin's Press.

African Development Bank 2003. *Selected Statistics on African Countries*. Abidjan: African Development Bank

Africa Human Rights Watch 2002. Ethiopia: Human Rights Developments. Africa Watch website (www.africawatch.org)

AIDA website: http//:aida.developmentgateway.org/

Amnesty International website, various years. www.amnesty.org

Andargachew Tiruneh 1993. *The Ethiopian Revolution 1974-1987*. Cambridge: Cambridge University Press.

APAP (Action Professionals' Association for the People), various years. Unpublished documents on human rights and human rights training. Addis Ababa, APAP

Asnake Kefale 2001. Regime Transition and Problems of Democratization in Post-insurgent African States: The Case of Ethiopia. Paper prepared for the 13th Biennial Conference of the African Association of Political Science, Yaounde, Cameroon, April.

Bahru Zewde and S. Pausewang (eds) 2002. *Ethiopia: The Challenge of Democracy from Below*. Uppsala: Nordiska Afrikainstitutet, and Addis Ababa: Forum for Social Studies.

Berhanu Nega 2000. The Media and Its Consumers in Ethiopia. Results from an Audience Survey. Paper prepared for the workshop The View From Below: Democratization and Governance in Ethiopia organized by Forum for Social Studies, Addis Ababa, 24-25 January.

Berhanu Nega and Meleskachew Ameha 2001. Report on the Media in the 2000 Elections in Ethiopia. Addis Ababa, Forum for Social Studies

Befekadu Degefe and Berhanu Nega (eds) 2000. *Annual Report on the Ethiopian Economy. Volume I 1999/2000*. Addis Ababa: Ethiopian Economic Association.

Befekadu Degefe, Berhanu Nega and Getahun Tafesse 2001. *Second Annual Report on the Ethiopian Economy Volume II 2000/2001*. Addis Ababa: Ethiopian Economic Association.

Brook Hailu 2000. Ethiopia in *Up In the Air? The State of Broadcasting in Eastern Africa*, Lynne Wanyeki, ed., London: Panos.

Canadian Embassy 2003. CIDA's DG [Democracy and Governance] Programme in Ethiopia. Unpublished report, Addis Ababa, 8 May

_____ 2004. Ethiopia: Country Development Programme Framework. Draft, Revised January. Addis Ababa.

Center for Capacity Building (2003), Civic Education in Ethiopia: Proceedings of a Workshop held on 6-8 May 2003, Addis Ababa

Central Statistical Authority 1999a. The 1994 Population and Housing Census of Ethiopia. Results at Country Level. Vol. II Analytical Report. Addis Ababa, June.

_____ 1999b. Statistical Report on the 1999 National Labor Force Survey. Addis Ababa, November.

Center for Local Capacity Building and Studies (CLCBS). 2003. Civic Education in Ethiopia: The Experience of Voter Education Activities prior to the May 2000 National Elections in Ethiopia, and Planning for the 2005 National Elections. Proceedings of the Workshop, May 6-9. Addis Ababa

Clapham, C. 1988. *Transformation and Continuity in Revolutionary Ethiopia.* Cambridge: Cambridge University Press.

Commission of the European Communities 2000. Communication from the commission on EU Election Assistance and Observation. Brussels.

Dessalegn Rahmato 1987. The Political Economy of Development in Ethiopia, in E. Keller and D. Rothschild (eds.) *Afro-Marxist Regimes: Ideology and Policy*, Boulder: Lynne Reinner.

_____ 1994. Neither Feast Nor Famine: Prospects for Food Security, in Abebe Zegeye and S. Pausewang (eds.), *Ethiopia in Change*, London: British Academic Press

_____ 2002. Civil Society Organizations in Ethiopia, in Bahru Zewde and S. Pausewang (eds.), *Ethiopia: The Challenge of Democracy from Below*, Uppsala: Nordiska Afrikainstituter and Addis Ababa: Forum for Social Studies.

_____ 2003a. Poverty and Agricultural Involution. In *Some Aspects of Poverty in Ethiopia: Three Selected Papers*, edited by Dessalegn Rahmato. FSS Studies on Poverty No. 1., Forum for Social Studies, Addis Ababa.

105

_____ 2003b. *Resettlement in Ethiopia. The Tragedy of Population Relocation in the 1980s*. FSS Discussion Paper No. 11, Forum for Social Studies, Addis Ababa.

_____ 'Civil Society Organizations in Ethiopia', Bahru Zewdie & Pausewang, Siegfried, eds. Ethiopia: The Challenge of Democracy from Below, Nordiska Afrikainstitutet and Forum for Social Studies, Stockholm: Elanders Gotab, 2002.

Dessalegn Rahmato and Aklilu Kidanu 2002. *Livelihood Insecurity among Urban Households in Ethiopia*. FSS Discussion Paper No. 8, Forum for Social Studies, Addis Ababa.

EEA (Ethiopian Economic Association) 2002. Impacts of the Ethio-Eritrean Border Conflict on the Performance of the Ethiopian Economy. Working Paper 3, Ethiopian Economic Research Institute, Addis Ababa, November.

EHRCO (Ethiopian Human Rights Council) 1999. *Compiled Reports of EHRCO (From December 1991 to December 1997)*. Addis Ababa, December.

_____ 2003. *Compiled Reports of EHRCO (Vol. II) From May 1997 to August 2003*. Addis Ababa, April.

_____The May 2000 General Election: A Report. 2002. Addis Ababa, Ethiopia.

EFJA (Ethiopian Free Press Journalists Association) 2003. Unpublished Reports on the Free Press. Addis Ababa

Ethiopian Women Lawyers Association (EWLA) 1997-1998. *Dimtsachen: A Newsletter of EWLA.*

_____ Various years. Research Documents.

_____ 1999. EWLA Activity Report 1996 - 2002. EWLA, Addis Ababa.

_____ 2000. *Berchi: The Journal of Ethiopian Women Lawyers Association*, 1,1, Summer

EC (European Commission) 2000. *ACP-EU Partnership Agreement signed in Cotonou on 23 June 2000*. Brussels: EC

Fambon, Samuel. 2003. 'The Funding of Elections and Political Parties in African States'. Africa Conference on Election, Democracy and Governance, 7-10 April, 2003. Pretoria

FAO (Food and Agricultural Organization) 2001. *The State of Food Insecurity in the World 2001*. Rome: FAO.

FDRE (Federal Democratic Republic of Ethiopia) 1995. *Constitution of the Federal Republic of Ethiopia*. Addis Ababa.

_____ 1999. Proclamation to Provide for the Systematic Management of Broadcasting Service. Proclamation 178/1999, *Negarit Gazeta*, Addis Ababa, June.

106

_____ 2000. Ethiopian Human Rights Commission Establishment Proclamation. No 210/2000, *Negarit Gazeta*, Addis Ababa, 4 July

_____ 2000. Institution of the Ombudsman Establishment Proclamation. No 211/2000, *Negarit Gazeta*, Addis Ababa, 24 July.

_____ 2001. Federal Ethics and Anti-Corruption Commission Establishment Proclamation. No. 235/2001, *Negarit Gazeta*, Addis Ababa, 24 May.

Federal Ethics and Anti-Corruption Commission) 2002-03. *Ethics* [Journal of FEAC], Volumes 1 and 2.

_____ 2003. The Commission's 18 Months (July 2001-December 2002) Performance Report. Presented to the EFDR Council of Peoples Representatives. Addis Ababa, January

Federal Supreme Court 2003. Activity Report and Training Schedule, March, Addis Ababa

Freedom House. Research methodology, copied from www.freedomhouse.org

Gilkes, P. 1975. *The Dying Lion: Feudalism and Modernization in Ethiopia.* London: St Martin's Press

John W. Harbeson. 2003. Elections and Democratization in Post-Mengistu Ethiopia', ed. Kumar, K. (ed) 1998. *Postconflict Elections, Democratization & International Assistance.* Lynne Reinner.

Human Rights Watch 2003. Ethiopia. Lessons in Repression: Violations of Academic Freedom in Ethiopia. Washington D.C.

Hyden, Goran 1997. Building Civil Society at the Turn of the Millennium. In J. Burbidge (ed), *Beyond Prince and Merchant. Citizen Participation and the Rise of Civil Society.* New York: PACT Publications

Inter-Africa Group, 'Capacity Building in Ethiopia: A Study of Impressions, NGO Networking Service, Addis Ababa, 1999-2000.

Inter-Parliamentary Union (IPU). 1993. Electoral Systems: A World-wide Comparative Study. Geneva

Kassahun Berhanu, 2003. 'Party Politics and Political Culture in Ethiopia', ed. Salih, Mohammed M.A., African Political Parties: Evolution, Institutionalisation and Governance, London: Pluto Press.

Kumar, K. (ed) 1998. *Postconflict Elections, Democratization & International Assistance.* Lynne Reinner.

107

Mairegu Bezabih 2003. *Ye-Gazetegnaneh Mouia* [The Profession of Journalism]. Addis Ababa: Mega Pubishing Co.

Mandefro Belay. May, 2002. 'Justice Reform Program: Preliminary Reform Profile, Program Contents and Objectives', Justice System Reform in Ethiopia: Proceedings of the Workshop on Ethiopia's Justice System Reform, Addis Ababa, Ethiopia.

Markakis, J. 1974. *Ethiopia: Anatomy of a Traditional Polity*. Oxford: Clarendon Press

Merera Gudina 2003. *Ethiopia: Competing Ethnic Nationalisms and the Quest for Democracy 1960-2000*. Addis Ababa: Chamber Printing House.

Ministry of Information 2002. *Ethiopia: The 2002 Year Book*. Addis Ababa

_____ 2003. Information from the Records of the Press Licensing and Regulation Department, Addis Ababa.

Ministry of Justice. May, 2002. Justice System Reform in Ethiopia: Proceedings of the Workshop on Ethiopia's Justice System Reform, Addis Ababa, Ethiopia.

Robert Nakamura. 2001. Final Report: Evaluation of UNDP Parliament Project 'Sustained Good Governance in Ethiopia Through Capacity-Building of the National Parliament'. Addis Ababa.

National Democratic Institute (NDI) and African-American Institute, 1992. *An Evaluation of the June 21, 1992 Elections in Ethiopia*, NDI, Washington, D.C.

National Electoral Board. July 2001. Overall Narrative and Financial Report of the Utilization of the Provisional Fund for Assistance to Political Parties for the 2000 National Elections of Ethiopia, Addis Ababa.

Norwegian Embassy 2003. Speech by the Ambassador, Mette Ravn, at a Seminar on Civil Society in Ethiopia, 27-28 May, Addis Ababa

_____ 2003. Information on Norwegian Assistance to Ethiopia provided by the First Secretary. Addis Ababa, December 13, 2003

OECD 2003. International Development Statistics. Electronic CD.

Ottaway, Marina 1999. *Africa's New Leaders: Democracy or State Reconstruction?* Washington, D.C.: Carnegie Endowment for International Peace.

Oyugi, Walter O.,. 2003 'The Link Between Resources and the Conduct of Elections in Africa', Africa Conference on

Election, Democracy and Governance, 7-10 April, 2003. Pretoria.

Pankhurst, Alula 2001. Returnees and Natural Resource Management. In Institutions of Natural Resource Management: Thematic Briefings, A. Pankhurst (ed.), Forum for Social Studies, Addis Ababa.

Pausewang, S. and K Tronvoll (eds) 2000. *The Ethiopian 2000 Elections. Democracy Advanced or Restricted.* University of Oslo.

Pausewang, S., K. Tronvoll and L.Aalen (eds) 2002. *Ethiopia since the Derg: A Decade of Democratic Pretension and Performance.* London: Zed Books

Polhemus, James 2002. An Action Plan for Useful Donor Involvement in Ethiopia's 2005 National Elections. Submitted to the Royal Netherlands Embassy. Addis Ababa.

Shimelis Bonsa 2000. *Survey of the Private Press in Ethiopia.* Forum for Social Studies

_____ 2002. The State of the Press in Ethiopia. In Bahru and Pausewang (eds.)

Shugarman, D. 2000. 'Combating Corruption: Regulating the Funding of Political Parties. 8th International Anti-Corruption Conference, IACC.

Tekeste Negash and K. Tronvoll 2000. *Brothers at War: Making Sense of the Eritrean-Ethiopian War.* James Currey

TGE (Transitional Government of Ethiopia) 1991. *The Transitional Charter of Ethiopia.* Addis Ababa, July.

_____.1995. Proclamation No. 111. A Proclamation to Establish the National Election Board of Ethiopia. Addis Ababa.

_____ 1992a. A Proclamation to Provide for the Freedom of the Press. Proclamation No. 34/1992, *Negarit Gazeta*, Addis Ababa, October.

_____ 1992b. *Ethiopia's Economic Policy During the Transition Period.* Addis Ababa, November

_____ 1993. Electoral Law of Ethiopia. Proclamation No. 64/1993, *Negarit Gazeta*, Addis Ababa.

Tronvoll, Kjetil and Aadland, 1995. The Process of Democratization in Ethiopia: An Expression of Popular Participation or Political Resistance? Human Rights Report No. 5, Norwegian Institute of Human Rights, Oslo

Tronvoll, K. 2000. *Ethiopia: A New Start?.* Minority Rights Group Report. London.

UNDP. www.undp.org

UNDP 2001. *A Four-Year Review and Analysis of Development Cooperation Activities of External Partners in Ethiopia.* Addis Ababa: UNDP

UNDP 2003a. Development Partnership in Ethiopia. Trends and Requirements for Reaching the PRSP & MDGs in Ethiopia 1997 to 2003. Unpublished report, UNDP-Ethiopia, Addis Ababa, May.

UNMEE. www.un.org/Depts/dpto/missions/unmee

_____ 2003b. *Human Development Report 2003.* New York: Oxford University Press

USAID Ethiopia various years and 2003 Briefing handouts: Strategic Objectives on Governance and Democratization (No 4 and No. 10). Fact Sheet on USAID Assistance to Ethiopia. Addis Ababa

U.S. State Department. February 2001. Bureau of Democracy, Human Rights, and Labor, Country Reports on Human Rights Practices. Washington, D.C.

U.S. Department of State 2003. Ethiopia. Country Reports on Human Rights Practices-2002. Washington, D.C., March 31.

Vestal, T. 2000. Ethiopia: A Post-Cold War African State. Westport, Ct: Praeger

WAAG Communications 2003. Opening Statement on 'The Journey of Press Freedom in Ethiopia (1992-2003)', present by WAAG Communications, Addis Ababa, 19 April.

Wanyeki, Lynne (ed) 2000. *Up in the Air? The State of Broadcasting in Eastern Africa.* London: PANOS

WFP (World Food Programme), various years. WFP website: www.wfp.org

World Bank 1999. *Ethiopia: Poverty Policies for the New Millennium.* Washington, D.C.: World Bank.

_____ 2000. *Ethiopia: Transitions in a Poor Economy.* Washington, D.C.: World Bank.

_____ 2002(?). Ethiopia: Emergency Recovery Project, An Overview. Unpublished paper, Addis Ababa, no date.

_____ 2003(?). Ethiopia: Public Expenditure Review. Volume I-Executive Summary and Overview. AFTP2, Africa Region. Washington, World Bank.

Newspapers Consulted

Government Papers
Addis Zemen (Main government daily- Amharic)

Ethiopian Herald (English daily)

Independent Papers
Addis Admas (Weekly- Amharic)
Addis Tribune (Weekly- English)
Addis Zena (Weekly- Amharic)
Menilik (Weekly- Amharic)
Reporter (Weekly- Amharic)
Tobya (Weekly- Amharic)

Persons Interviewed

Abera Haile Mariam, Senior Staff, APAP, Addis Ababa, 18 July 2003
Abebe Taye, Public Relations and Documentation Officer, EHRCO, 21 July 2003
Akalewold Bantirgu, Coordinator, CRDA IMP and NePRAD Departments, 21 August 2003.
Ammanuel Abdissa, Senior Staff Member, Mass Media Training Institute, Addis Ababa, 8 August 2003
Amare Aregawi, Chief Editor, *Reporter* Newspaper, Addis Ababa, 23 July 2003
Assefa Birru, General Manager, National Election Board, Addis Ababa, 28 July 2003
Ms Azeb Haile Sellasie, Expert, Press Licensing and Regulatory Department, Ministry of Information, Addis Ababa, 6 August 2003.
Bekele Alemu, Governance Unit, CIDA, Canadian Embassy, Addis Ababa, 30 September 2003
Oliver Blake, Governance Advisor, DFID, Addis Ababa, 28 August 2003.
Desta Tesfaye, Deputy Manager, Ethiopian Broadcasting Agency, Addis Ababa, 19 August 2003
Goldbeck, Brian, Counselor, Political and Economic Affairs, US Embassy, Addis Ababa, 4 December 2003
Hailu Shawel, President, All Ethiopia Unity Party, 24 July 2003
Jalal Abdle Latif, Executive Director, InterAfrica Group, Addis Ababa, 21 July 2003
Kifle Mulat, President, Ethiopian Free Press Association, 15 August 2003
Ledetu Ayalew, Secretary General, Ethiopian Democratic Party (EDP), 18 July 2003

Mekonnen Wondimneh, Expert, Civic Education and Training, and Acting Head, NEB, Political Parties Registration. July 28, 2003.

Mandefro Belay, Director, Judicial Reform Program, 28 July 2003.

Melaku Tegegne, Director, PANOS Ethiopia, Addis Ababa, 20 August 2003

Meselkachew Amha, Editor, *Addis Zena* Newspaper, 18 August 2003

Janet Mortitz, Program Specialist, UNDP, Addis Ababa, on several occasions in August and September 2003

Ms *Original Wolde Giorgis,* Legal Advisor, EWLA, Speech to Workshop on Gender and the Law, 15 August 2003

James Polhemus, Former Head of Governance Department, USAID-Ethiopia, Oral Information, Addis Ababa, 17 May 2003

Inge H. Rydland, Deputy Head of Mission, Norwegian Embassy, Addis Ababa, 28 May 2003

Saheleselassie Abebe, General Manager, Center for Local Capacity Building and Studies, 5 August 2003.

Taye Belachew, Journalist and Head of Publications, *Tobya* Newspaper, Addis Ababa, 11 July 2003

Teferi Asfaw, Public Relations Officer, Addis Ababa Chamber of Commerce, and Project Coordinator, **Vote Addis Project**, 2000/01 Elections.

Teferi Wossen, Manager, WAAG Communications, Addis Ababa, 22 August 2003

Teshager Asfaw, Commercial and Political Officer, Netherlands Embassy, Addis Ababa, 19 August 2003

Wolfram Vetter, Second Secretary (Political Affairs), Delegation of the European Commission in Ethiopia, Addis Ababa, 5 September 2003

Cecil Vink, Second Secretary, Netherlands Embassy, Addis Ababa, 19 August 2003

Laura Williams, Second Secretary, British Embassy, Addis Ababa, 28 August 2003

Ms Yetenayet Andarge, Staff member, EWLA, Addis Ababa, 20 August 2003

FSS PUBLICATIONS LIST

FSS Newsletter

Medrek (Quarterly since 1998. English and Amharic)

FSS Discussion Papers

No. 1. *Water Resource Development in Ethiopia: Issues of Sustainability and Participation.* Dessalegn Rahmato. June 1999

No. 2. *The City of Addis Ababa: Policy Options for the Governance and Management of a City with Multiple Identity.* Meheret Ayenew. December 1999

No. 3. *Listening to the Poor: A Study Based on Selected Rural and Urban Sites in Ethiopia.* Aklilu Kidanu and Dessalegn Rahmato. May 2000

No. 4. *Small-Scale Irrigation and Household Food Security. A Case Study from Central Ethiopia.* Fuad Adem. February 2001

No. 5. *Land Redistribution and Female-Headed Households.* By Yigremew Adal. November 2001

No. 6. *Environmental Impact of Development Policies in Peripheral Areas: The Case of Metekel, Northwest Ethiopia.* Wolde-Selassie Abbute. Forthcoming, 2001

No. 7. *The Environmental Impact of Small-scale Irrigation: A Case Study.* Fuad Adem. Forthcoming, 2001

No. 8. *Livelihood Insecurity Among Urban Households in Ethiopia.* Dessalegn Rahmato and Aklilu Kidanu. October 2002

No. 9. *Rural Poverty in Ethiopia: Household Case Studies from North Shewa.* Yared Amare. December 2002

No.10. *Rural Lands in Ethiopia: Issues, Evidences and Policy Response.* Tesfaye Teklu. May 2003

No.11. *Resettlement in Ethiopia: The Tragedy of Population Relocation in the 1980s.* Dessalegn Rahmato. June 2003

FSS Monograph Series

No. 1. *Survey of the Private Press in Ethiopia: 1991-1999.*
Shimelis Bonsa. 2000

No. 2. *Environmental Change and State Policy in Ethiopia: Lessons from Past Experience.* Dessalegn Rahmato. 2001

FSS Conference Proceedings

1. *Issues in Rural Development. Proceedings of the Inaugural Workshop of the Forum for Social Studies, 18 September 1998.* Edited by Zenebework Taddesse. 2000

2. *Development and Public Access to Information in Ethiopia.* Edited by Zenebework Tadesse. 2000

3. *Environment and Development in Ethiopia.* Edited by Zenebework Tadesse. 2001

4. *Food Security and Sustainable Livelihoods in Ethiopia.* Edited by Yared Amare. 2001

5. *Natural Resource Management in Ethiopia.* Edited by Alula Pankhurst. 2001

6. *Poverty and Poverty Policy in Ethiopia.* Special issue containing the papers of FSS' final conference on poverty held on 8 March 2002

Consultation Papers on Poverty

No. 1. *The Social Dimensions of Poverty.* Papers by Minas Hiruy, Abebe Kebede, and Zenebework Tadesse. Edited by Meheret Ayenew. June 2001

No. 2. *NGOs and Poverty Reduction.* Papers by Fassil W. Mariam, Abowork Haile, Berhanu Geleto, and Jemal Ahmed. Edited by Meheret Ayenew. July 2001

No. 3. *Civil Society Groups and Poverty Reduction.* Papers by Abonesh H. Mariam, Zena Berhanu, and Zewdie Shitie. Edited by Meheret Ayenew. August 2001

No. 4.   *Listening to the Poor*. Oral Presentation by Gizachew Haile, Senait Zenawi, Sisay Gessesse and Martha Tadesse. In Amharic. Edited by Meheret Ayenew. November 2001

No.5.   *The Private Sector and Poverty Reduction [Amharic]*. Papers by Teshome Kebede, Mullu Solomon and Hailemeskel Abebe. Edited by Meheret Ayenew, November 2001

No.6.   *Government, Donors and Poverty Reduction*. Papers by H.E. Ato Mekonnen Manyazewal, William James Smith and Jeroen Verheul. Edited by Meheret Ayenew, February 2002.

No.7.   *Poverty and Poverty Policy in Ethiopia*. Edited by Meheret Ayenew, 2002

Books

1.   *Ethiopia: The Challenge of Democracy from Below*. Edited by Bahru Zewde and Siegfried Pausewang. Nordic African Institute, Uppsala and the Forum for Social Studies, Addis Ababa. 2002

Special Publications

Thematic Briefings on Natural Resource Management, Enlarged Edition. Edited by Alula Pankhurst. Produced jointly by the Forum for Social Studies and the University of Sussex. January 2001

New Series

• **Gender Policy Dialogue Series**

No. 1   *Gender and Economic Policy*. Edited by Zenebework Tadesse. March 2003

No. 2   *Gender and Poverty (Amharic)*. Edited by Zenebework Tadesse. March 2003

No. 3   *Gender and Social Development in Ethiopia*. (Forthcoming).

No. 4   *Gender Policy Dialogue in Oromiya Region*. Edited by Eshetu Bekele. September 2003

- **Consultation Papers on Environment**

No. 1   *Environment and Environmental Change in Ethiopia.* Edited by Gedion Asfaw. Consultation Papers on Environment. March 2003

No. 2   *Environment, Poverty and Gender.* Edited by Gedion Asfaw. Consultation Papers on Environment. May 2003

No. 3   *Environmental Conflict.* Edited by Gedion Asfaw. Consultation Papers on Environment. July 2003

No. 4   *Economic Development and its Environmental Impact.* Edited by Gedion Asfaw. Consultation Papers on Environment. August 2003

No. 5   *Government ad Environmental Policy.* Consultation Papers on Environment. January 2004

- **FSS Studies on Poverty**

No. 1   *Some Aspects of Poverty in Ethiopia: Three Selected Papers.* Papers by Dessalegn Rahmato, Meheret Ayenew and Aklilu Kidanu. Edited by Dessalegn Rahmato. March 2003.

No. 2   *Faces of Poverty: Life in Gäta, Wälo.* By Harald Aspen. June 2003.

No. 3   *Destitution in Rural Ethiopia.* By Yared Amare. August 2003

www.ingramcontent.com/pod-product-compliance
Lightning Source LLC
Chambersburg PA
CBHW021833020426
42334CB00014B/607